MY OWN WORST ENEMY

A Black Man's American Story

Thank God for every single obstacle, each of them built up
my endurance to run this marathon we call life.

ISMAEL R. BROWN

Cover Design by Brandon B. Hamilton

My Own Worst Enemy
A Black Man's American Story

By Ismael R. Brown

ISBN (Trade Paperback)   978-0-9987937-0-2
ISBN (Kindle eBook)   978-0-9987937-1-9
ISBN (iPad/Nook eBook)   978-0-9987937-2-6

Printed in the United States of America

I dedicate this book to every person who feels incapable of self-love—those of you who lack the proper guidance needed to excel past your overwhelming surroundings of fear, distrust, and scarcity of positive reinforcement. Just know nothing lasts forever, and you will make it through. I am a testament to discovering the meaning of "I love me."

I would also like to dedicate this book to everyone who has survived my growing pains throughout the years. Your commitment to my development speaks volumes to the pureness of your hearts. I cannot thank you enough.

God to order his footsteps, is a provider, and is not
s for betterment of self and the people around him.
E, we get a glimpse of how he forged his own rite of .
oped these axioms. MOWE allows us to see Ish on
d how the "boxing in" of the black male leaves him
ooking for answers.

ate. As a young black male who "made it out," I still
pressure from the outside world not to fulfill cultural
ve tried to make all the "right" moves. I attended
d law school, and became a lawyer. In spite of my
s, I still experience a sinking feeling of not belonging
mmunity at times because people close to me have
periences than I do. The experiences of the black
so unreal, so unfathomable that even clear video-
oes not sway others to believe our truth and reality.
unity has a long, unwritten list of rules that I, and
ituated, have to abide by or else risk everything—an

ok too menacing or threatening.
smile on your face.
ppropriately."
oper" English.
ny other arbitrary rules for survival.

jority of these rules from my mother. As a child, I
he worried for me all the time. You see, what I did
as a child—which I now do as a man—is the wages
k man in America is death. And these high stakes
le black family. Abide by these rules and you may
gh to go to college, have a family, and watch your
aybe. It is that maybe that kept my mother vigilant.
me of us can put aside this reality for a moment to
f happiness.

CONTENTS

FOREWORD
MOWE is o

one who allows
afraid to take ris
Through MOW
passage and deve
his own path an
exasperated and

I can rel
feel unrelenting
stereotypes. I ha
college, graduate
accomplishment
to my larger cor
very different ex
community are
taped evidence
The black comm
others similarly
untimely death:

Don't l
Have a
Dress "a
Talk "p
And ma

WHAT IS A MAN?
ROCKY AND TANGLE
of passage that track this j
riage rites, and death rites.
ing a leap from one stage
some rites of passage may
of New Zealand traditiona
adulthood with facial tatto
tribe of the Brazilian Ama:
let ants and endure the an
Aborigines in Australia ha
knocked out. They are ther
community, circumcised, a
out chewing. They go hunt
they are covered in blood
passage is their "man birth."

No matter how od
the community come toget
act as a guide and a resour
exists for an adolescent bla
"man birth"? American bla
defined path. We often sw
the right path. Some find th

Ish was a man with
teetering on the brink on m
for this foreword, I asked Is

I learned the m
wondered why
not understand
for being a bla
affect every sing
make it far eno
kids grow. Just
It is a wonder s
share a glimpse

I met Ish on the heels of his breakup of a romantic relationship. He was despondent but still exuded a quiet resilience. That is what drew me to him. We became fast friends. I later learned Ish is not one who shares his emotions, but I started to tell him my stories, *the stories of the rose that grew from concrete*, as Tupac wrote. The more I talked, the more he listened, and the more we realized how much our stories paralleled. And that is what leads me here, writing this foreword. I am positive many more stories abound from our mothers and fathers, brothers and sisters, sons and daughters. The similarities in our dark stories put us in a grim fraternity. We pledge this fraternity simply by walking the streets in the immutable characteristic of our black skin. Some of you will read this and make the mistake of thinking the days of being targeted simply because of skin color are over. To such readers, I challenge you to make a concerted effort to open your heart to feeling this experience. From slavery to Jim Crow to redlining to the systematic denial of bank loans to police brutality—black folk continue to have a tough time. This book is not meant to illicit pity, but to enlighten, inform, and encourage.

When Ish approached me to write this foreword, it was a project I knew I had to be a part of. Whether or not this book makes it on any best sellers list, it is my hope it reaches someone who needs it. Someone who feels trapped within his or her own skin as many of our ancestors felt before us. I pray MOWE inspires someone to reach out of the trenches of victimhood and into the great beyond of possibilities. I pray my words resonate as clearly as if I were in the same room with you engaging in conversation. This is my prayer for you.

I won't paint the picture that all is lost. The community has positive spots dotting areas the entire world has given up on. The community needs its stories told. MOWE is the story of Ish. Thousands more Ishes have stories, but they do not have the opportunity to tell them. Keep that in mind as you traverse the pages of this book. This is an opportunity to lift up and celebrate the achievements of the community while acknowledging its pain. While difficult, it is cathartic to recognize a successful and growing rose of a desolate wasteland.

MOWE is the experience of the community. MOWE is the story of Ish. MOWE is our story!

– **Reshad Favors**, Esq.

WHO IS THE ENEMY?

THE ENEMY: *A man endures and exhibits no pain. It is a sign of weakness to display any type of emotion. It's about finding your way and rejecting any signs of help because a man stands on his own. Never let someone feel as if you owe him or her anything. It's a concrete jungle out there, survival of the fittest. You're either at the table or on the menu.*

I WAS BORN ISMAEL RASHID BROWN, THE BEARER OF THE CRACKED, TARNISHED CROWN. A crown fitted for someone without compassion, clemency or even conscious of how his iniquities affected those around him. A crown only worthy of a double-minded man who repudiated the purest form of endearment that is love—all the while yearning for it in silence. The inability to articulate the desire for the very shunned love only hardened the heart of the silent bearer. This crown could only be placed on the head of someone blind to the realities of being grateful for the current state of life versus seeing how drastically worse things could be. A crown consisting of an overflow of ungratefulness is more fitting. The price of sporting a crown without honor or dignity came at the expense of those fearless enough to love the unlovable. Or maybe they were exemplifying the definition of insanity—wanting to love someone who again and again showed them the unchanging result of how incapable he was to reciprocate.

The crown was light with responsibility, but heavy in the guilt that accumulated from abandoning the people who needed him. Never taking the initiative to pick up the phone to ask how they were doing, to see if they needed anything, or just simply to say hello.

Effort is a word that did not exist in my realm of relationships; I was too consumed with building the empire bound for a devastating demise. This crown was not placed upon my head from my biological father like most dynasties throughout history. I earned this crown from years of blinding anger, altering my perception of life itself, not trusting anyone, and rejecting all forms of handouts—which I viewed as a sign of weakness. Asking for them was soft, and being soft will get you taken advantage of or killed. I thought the key to unlocking the door to manhood meant that if I needed anything, I would venture into the world and take it—whether "taking it" materialized in the form of being an overachiever at school, active in corporate America, or punching the clock on the pavement that Uncle Sam owned. That very pavement where the blood of Cain and Abel's descendants spilled nightly over the most trivial issues. It was all that I saw on TV and in movies that I thoroughly enjoyed, like *Boyz In Da Hood, Poetic Justice, New Jack City, Lean On Me, Menace II Society*. Even my ears were submerged in the violence destroying people of color, through the vivid lyrics of my favorite rap artists.

I couldn't get enough of how they used the instrumental as their easel, and their metaphors served as paintbrush strokes creating a masterpiece of genocide. These forms of entertainment depicted the socioeconomic travesty destroying hope in black communities.

This crown gave me the undeniable power to believe in me over all. It just pulsated with confidence. As the bearer of this crown, I was known as the emperor of the Bleeding Kingdom of Self. I was a dictator of one, king of a twisted psyche. I was not elected by a governing body, nor was I a great warrior who fought tirelessly for his people; if anything, I was a mass murderer of relationships. There was blood all over my hands. Some of it dried from previous massacres while the rest was still warm and moist from new blood I spilled, destroying all hope of cultivating any form of a relationship. I spent 20 odd years building this kingdom from the ground up. Brick by brick I built it, and it was mine to be proud of. I never saw any form of wrongdoing in being the ruler of self until the blood surrounding my barely standing throne became my own. I began to notice the hand I had in sabotaging the very things I wanted in life. A relationship with my father, a beautiful girlfriend whom I'd one day wed, and inseparable bonds with friends I could rely on no matter the situation. But none of this would come to pass. I destroyed it all, feeling incomplete and empty with only my crown to show for it all.

I grew weaker with each passing year as the carrier of this crown. Headaches became more frequent, the stress more severe, and the tactics I previously deployed to victory became useless as I was losing multiple battles. My kingdom was under siege. I was now battling the reflection I could barely see. The battlefield became unfamiliar. I was warring with self; and with each soul I sent to God was a piece of me dying. My head was bleeding, bruised, and pale—just as described in the poem "The Test of a Man." My back was against the wall and no help was coming. I could fight no longer, for death was eminent. The bleeding kingdom of self had to fall in order to discover the root of my selfishness, distaste for people, and apprehensiveness to love. I am Ismael Rashid Brown, and this is my canvas.

A canvas illuminating the moments and feelings I hide from everyone in the dawn when the night is darkest before day. This is an introspective look into the piss-poor ideology that got me absolutely nowhere in life, except lost in a world full of poor choices. I've exhibited every possible character flaw with flying colors: a hypocrite, a self-centered fool, a judgmental jerk, a habitual liar, and my favorite of them all, a closed-minded ingrate. Correcting these bruising character imperfections was not a prerogative; they were merely the opinions of people around me, and healing their opinions wasn't on my to-do list either. But I was wrong; these people only reciprocated what I disseminated. I believed I could actually live without sustaining any meaningful connections to other human beings. That falsehood demonstrated my lack of understanding for running the marathon of life. The bible tells us of the importance of community in 1 John 4:11, *"Dear Friends, since God so loved us, we also ought to love one another."* Or in Romans 12:16, *"Live in harmony with one another, Do not be proud, but willing to associate with people of low position. Do not be conceited."* I was the antithesis of these verses, formulating dissonance with my own creator. Even God's blueprint and Living Word couldn't convince me of the need for harmonious living with people.

> *I swear don't need anyone in life, I got me!*
> *I came in the world alone…I'll die alone, too.*

My mindset growing up as a child and the early part of adulthood was fixated on the idea that I was in control of my life. All I had to do was work hard and whatever I put my mind to was achievable. I was the poster child of the bootstrap theory that a person optimizes and gives himself the best opportunities by creating his own and lifting himself up by his bootstraps—as introduced by author Horatio Alger. He wrote novels generating the idea of making something out

I met Ish on the heels of his breakup of a romantic relationship. He was despondent but still exuded a quiet resilience. That is what drew me to him. We became fast friends. I later learned Ish is not one who shares his emotions, but I started to tell him my stories, *the stories of the rose that grew from concrete,* as Tupac wrote. The more I talked, the more he listened, and the more we realized how much our stories paralleled. And that is what leads me here, writing this foreword. I am positive many more stories abound from our mothers and fathers, brothers and sisters, sons and daughters. The similarities in our dark stories put us in a grim fraternity. We pledge this fraternity simply by walking the streets in the immutable characteristic of our black skin. Some of you will read this and make the mistake of thinking the days of being targeted simply because of skin color are over. To such readers, I challenge you to make a concerted effort to open your heart to feeling this experience. From slavery to Jim Crow to redlining to the systematic denial of bank loans to police brutality—black folk continue to have a tough time. This book is not meant to illicit pity, but to enlighten, inform, and encourage.

When Ish approached me to write this foreword, it was a project I knew I had to be a part of. Whether or not this book makes it on any best sellers list, it is my hope it reaches someone who needs it. Someone who feels trapped within his or her own skin as many of our ancestors felt before us. I pray MOWE inspires someone to reach out of the trenches of victimhood and into the great beyond of possibilities. I pray my words resonate as clearly as if I were in the same room with you engaging in conversation. This is my prayer for you.

I won't paint the picture that all is lost. The community has positive spots dotting areas the entire world has given up on. The community needs its stories told. MOWE is the story of Ish. Thousands more Ishes have stories, but they do not have the opportunity to tell them. Keep that in mind as you traverse the pages of this book. This is an opportunity to lift up and celebrate the achievements of the community while acknowledging its pain. While difficult, it is cathartic to recognize a successful and growing rose of a desolate wasteland.

MOWE is the experience of the community. MOWE is the story of Ish. MOWE is our story!

– **Reshad Favors**, Esq.

CONTENTS

FOREWORD
MOWE is our story!

WHAT IS A MAN? THE ROAD TO MANHOOD IS A ROCKY AND TANGLED JOURNEY. World cultures have rites of passage that track this journey—birth rites, initiation rites, marriage rites, and death rites. All mark a man's progression in life, making a leap from one stage to another. From the outside looking in, some rites of passage may seem bizarre. Young native Maori males of New Zealand traditionally marked the passage from boyhood to adulthood with facial tattoos. To become a man in the Satere-Mawe tribe of the Brazilian Amazon, a boy must wear a glove full of bullet ants and endure the ants' painful stings. Boys of the Mardudjara Aborigines in Australia have their septum pierced and front tooth knocked out. They are then taken into the wilderness by men of the community, circumcised, and expected to ingest the foreskin without chewing. They go hunting and return with food to camp, where they are covered in blood to symbolize their manhood. This rite of passage is their "man birth."

No matter how odd, these ceremonies have utility. Men of the community come together and usher boys into manhood. They act as a guide and a resource to these boys. But what rite of passage exists for an adolescent black male in the U.S. on the path to his "man birth"? American black males most often grow up without a defined path. We often swerve in high speed in an attempt to find the right path. Some find the right one; others perish in fiery crashes.

Ish was a man without a defined path. His story was one of teetering on the brink on many fiery crashes. While developing ideas for this foreword, I asked Ish, "What is a man?" Ish defines a man as one who allows God to order his footsteps, is a provider, and is not afraid to take risks for betterment of self and the people around him. Through MOWE, we get a glimpse of how he forged his own rite of passage and developed these axioms. MOWE allows us to see Ish on his own path and how the "boxing in" of the black male leaves him exasperated and looking for answers.

I can relate. As a young black male who "made it out," I still feel unrelenting pressure from the outside world not to fulfill cultural stereotypes. I have tried to make all the "right" moves. I attended college, graduated law school, and became a lawyer. In spite of my accomplishments, I still experience a sinking feeling of not belonging to my larger community at times because people close to me have very different experiences than I do. The experiences of the black community are so unreal, so unfathomable that even clear video-taped evidence does not sway others to believe our truth and reality. The black community has a long, unwritten list of rules that I, and others similarly situated, have to abide by or else risk everything—an untimely death:

> Don't look too menacing or threatening.
> Have a smile on your face.
> Dress "appropriately."
> Talk "proper" English.
> And many other arbitrary rules for survival.

I learned the majority of these rules from my mother. As a child, I wondered why she worried for me all the time. You see, what I did not understand as a child—which I now do as a man—is the wages for being a black man in America is death. And these high stakes affect every single black family. Abide by these rules and you may make it far enough to go to college, have a family, and watch your kids grow. Just maybe. It is that maybe that kept my mother vigilant. It is a wonder some of us can put aside this reality for a moment to share a glimpse of happiness.

of nothing. The outline of the American Dream was conceptualized through his literary works such as *Ragged Dick*. This theory was engraved in my mind. I inhaled the idea, spoke about the idea, dreamt about it, and prematurely tasted the rewards of achieving success on my own. But on the contrary, I was raised up in the church and heard the Word of God. Yet I failed to understand who was truly in control. So time after time, I would find myself disappointed in the results of my actions. I allowed my thoughts to succumb to my constant failures more so than the small victories I'd achieved.

I didn't rest on the fact I was human and that these were common hurdles of life everyone was bound to go through at some point in time. I didn't relate to the makeup of most humans, requiring love and companionship. I refused all of that, pushing people away who cared. Loving anyone long enough only grew into unexpected hurt. The identical hurt we try to avoid at all cost. The exact hurt tainting your heart, hindering you from reciprocating similar emotions. Yes, the same hurt they said they'd never inflict upon you because they said they…loved you.

Someone like me couldn't define love; I was too full of unforgiving rage, mad at everyone in sight. Truthfully, I hated people. They were too unpredictable, lacked accountability, and all about self-preservation. People were like revolving doors, constantly entering and exiting my life. I didn't trust people. The abandonment I felt was real. I never expected them to stay around long, so I felt no need to build rapport with them.

People reminded me of how dysfunctional I was. We were merely reflections of one another. Half of us more willing to uncover our unstableness and not too afraid to say, "Hey, I messed up, my mistake." But that wasn't me. I was part of the other half who never accounted for their wrongs, simply blaming all problems and unfair circumstances on others. As a result, I was overly critical of people creating unrealistic or unobtainable expectations. Failure was the only outcome they could achieve in my eyes. I wasn't biased, though

I applied this same principle to my own life. This demented precept has continuously haunted me from the child I was to the adult I am today. The self-implied pressure was worse by far than what I placed on people. Why? Honestly, I don't know why I'm so hard on myself. It's a truth whose reason I've yet to discover.

My heart was frozen, colder than a subzero freezer, incapable of beating for love. A combination of troubling life experiences and being spoon-fed self-hatred by my country made me worse. A time came when I, as a believer in God, doubted him, feeling punished and even cursed for being born black.

I was born in America, *the land of the free*, where the Declaration of Independence reads, "We hold these truths to be self-evident, that all men are created equal, that they are endowed by their Creator with certain unalienable Rights, that among these are Life, Liberty and the pursuit of Happiness." Thomas Jefferson, widely known as a slave owner, was the principal author of this doctrine of subjective freedom that is the cornerstone of this nation. Take the time to digest the paradox of a prominent slave owner professing all men are created equal. Since the establishment of this nation, it's evident that equality does not pertain to everyone who calls this nation home. Yet just a few years later in 1781, in Thomas Jefferson's book *Notes on the State of Virginia*, he compared Africans to Anglo-Saxons, concluding:

> To our reproach it must be said, that though for a century and a half we have had under our eyes the races of black and of red men, they have never yet been viewed by us as subjects of natural history. I advance it therefore as a suspicion only, that the blacks, whether originally a distinct race, or made distinct by time and circumstances, are inferior to the whites in the endowments both of body and mind. It is not against experience to suppose, that different species of the same genus, or varieties of the same species, may possess different qualifications.[1]

So let me rephrase: I was born In America, *the land of the* un*free*, where Africans were displaced during the early 1600s to late 1800s and suffered from barbaric slavery in which men were stripped of their humanity, women degraded and savagely raped, and children were taken from the loving arms of their mothers.

The infamous *Willie Lynch Letter & Making of a Slave* speech of 1712 outlined and detailed the greatest blueprint for African-American oppression that is still prevalent in 2016. Lynch, a British slave owner in the West Indies, explained the economics of properly enslaving blacks by destroying their psyche and family foundation. I must give credit where it is due; Lynch was a remarkable theorist and he knew it by saying, "In my bag here, I have a foolproof method for controlling your black slaves. I guarantee every one of you that if installed correctly, it will control the slaves for at least 300 years."[2] His elementary yet effective plan consisted of polarizing the differences amongst black slaves and subcategorizing those variations against one another. For example, he pitted old males vs. young males, light skin vs. dark skin, and males vs. females. This was psychological warfare against an ill prepared people. These fabricated conflicts created mass distrust and inferiority within the black community.

These commonly buried, overlooked realities have become an unacknowledged afterthought for America. Yes, we should move on and let the past remain just as it is, the past. But until this country unifies as a whole, the underlying hate and division will continue to flourish throughout the land, the 50 states of America.

America would come to teach Africans this land would never be theirs and would find other ways to systematically hinder any progression. Abraham Lincoln, America's 16th President, championed the passing of the Emancipation Proclamation of 1863, generating a sense of optimism that equality was coming, the same equality guaranteed per the Declaration of Independence. However, this edict would be the first of many instances in which this country sells people of color a false sense of advancement. Yet it became a reminder that the fate of Africans was subject to the hands of a white man who feared blacks and also did not believe in their capabilities. Lincoln went on to say, "There is a physical difference between the White and Black race. There must be the position of superior or inferior, and I as much as any man am in favor of having the superior assigned to the White race."[3] Lincoln proved, more than anything else, to be another hypocritical leader who disavowed inequality amongst races while promoting the concepts of white privilege.

The hands of slaves built this land, yet restitution for the decades of mistreatment never came to fruition. The allocation of 40 acres and a mule for all the anguish ended with Andrew Johnson, the nation's 17th President. However, let me remind you that this nation has handed reparations to other groups of mistreated people— Native and Japanese Americans.

The true indigenous people of this nation—Native Americans or Indians, as wrongly named by Christopher Columbus who thought he had landed in the East Indies instead of the Americas— may have endured the worst type of havoc from European settlers. These explorers of the New World brought with them diseases that the immune systems and herbal medicines of the natives could not protect against. As a result, the casualties of indigenous people would claim entire tribes, driving down their populations drastically. Additionally, westward expansion brought over a conqueror's mindset. Ownership of the land became an unresolvable issue amongst both sides.

Violence ensued as Europeans slaughtered natives by the hundreds with their advanced weaponry. In time, with the formation of North America, these peoples would continue to fall within the crosshairs of land hungry pirates known as government. President Andrew Jackson signed the Indian Removal Act on May 28, 1830. The ancestral lands of Indians within newly created state borders were seized in exchange for unsettled lands west of the Mississippi.

This act resulted in the death of 4,000 Indians on the forced journey known as the Trail of Tears.[4]

Native Americans were plagued with illnesses, stripped of their lands, murdered when resisting the development of dear America, and forced to assimilate for survival, which depended on their ability to look and act accordingly—meaning, as white as possible. America grew compassionate for the pain it had caused—a theme of repentance that would recur again and again in our nation's history—by saying we're sorry in the form of cash stipends, ungoverned land, and free education guaranteed through educational waivers. Why hasn't the black community received these same allotments? African slaves built America. Yet today's black community is still taught to hate one another, resulting in fratricide, which is polarized by the media.

Then on February 19, 1942, just ten weeks after the attack on Pearl Harbor, President Franklin Roosevelt signed Executive Order 9066, authorizing the forcible removal of all American citizens of Japanese ancestry to be placed in interment camps.[5] The treatment of these American citizens was harsh, unfair, and as you can imagine, inhumane. But during times of war, compassion has no place, and only diplomatic strokes of ego reign supreme. Roosevelt made the wrong decision, and amends wouldn't be made until nearly 40 years later with President Ronald Reagan signing of the Civil Liberties Act, which paid $20,000 in reparations to more than 100,000 survivors of these internment camps. I guess $20,000 was the magic number required to erase memories of the traumatic experiences that plagued childhoods and the mental stability of adults. But why the audacity to take 40 years to say you're sorry? America, America, America…the nerve you and your publicly elected officials have.

I've said I was born In America, *the land of the* un*free*—where Negroes were pictured on the front pages of newspapers, swinging from the branches of oak trees like unpickable low hanging fruit. Their bodies chilling as the warmth of life escaped through their pores. The last images of these unfortunate souls would show crowds of whites gathered to bare witness to their deaths, praying for forgiveness and hoping their lives would be spared. But no, there would be no reasoning or understanding for whatever accusations resulted from the kicking of feet grasping for an object to rest upon as the noose tightened around necks. I must warn you of a people's pain that is no longer about being suffocated by noose to death but more about the American flag that still claims the lives of the same unfavored black people in the 21st century.

The forms of attack on blacks has progressively changed over time. In the southern part of America, Jim Crow laws were created to promote segregation in which separate never equated to equal. Everything the Negroes were relegated to was of lower class and poorer conditions—from restaurants to schoolhouses. The one place where we needed equality above all else was in the classroom. How desperately did our people need to be educated? It was as imperative as the oxygen in our lungs. The 1960s South became lynching grounds for the Ku Klux Klan, which reigned supreme. According to Title VIII, section 802—Strengthening the Criminal Laws Against Terrorism, of the Uniting and Strengthening America by Providing Appropriate Tools Required to Intercept and Obstruct Terrorism Act (commonly known as the USA Patriot Act), domestic terrorism is defined as:

> (A) involve acts dangerous to human life that are a violation of the criminal laws of the United States or of any State;
> (B) appear to be intended –
> > i. to intimidate or coerce a civilian population;
> > ii. to influence the policy of a government by intimidation or coercion; or
> > iii. to affect the conduct of a government by mass destruction, assassination, or kidnapping; and
> (C) occur primarily within the territorial jurisdiction of the United States[6].

It's just too bad this act wasn't passed until 2001, long after these white sheet hooded cowards succeeded in their efforts to incite fear, kidnap, intimidate, and assassinate the civilian population of people of color.

The attack on blacks extended beyond the hatred of these southern white men who burned crosses and rode stallion like horses in the night to the Oval Office in the West Wing. Former Nixon domestic policy chief John Ehrlichman, from his own mouth, told Dan Baum, writer for Harper, "The Nixon campaign in 1968, and the Nixon White House after that, had two enemies: antiwar left and black people." He continued on to say, "You understand what I'm saying? We knew we couldn't make it illegal to be either against the war or black, but by getting the public to associate the hippies with marijuana and blacks with heroin. And then criminalizing both heavily, we could disrupt those communities. We could arrest their leaders, raid their homes, break up their meetings, and vilify them night after night on the evening news. Did we know we were lying about the drugs? Of course we did."[7] This isn't shocking by any means. John Ehrlichman simply gave validity to what all blacks already knew—America had set blacks in its sights and would do whatever it took to destroy all hope.

When I reflect back on my own grade-school curriculum, I realize the school system failed me. The extent of black history covered only the institution of slavery, Dr. Martin Luther King and the Civil Rights movement, and Malcolm X's militancy in demanding justice. And of course, we all know how those stories ended—in the death of our most decorated leaders. Let me backtrack for a minute. The history books of my grade-school years between 1995-2009 also polarized the major sporting figures of African descent, legends like Joe Louis, Jesse Owens, Jackie Robinson, and Satchel Page. All these men of prestigious stature deserved more than the few paragraphs given in my history books. I also couldn't understand why sports figures were revered more than our educated, thought-provoking African American leaders and orators. These leaders included figures like Marcus Garvey, W. E .B. Du Bois, Frederick Douglas, Edward Brooke, Stokley Carmichael, Booker T. Washington, Dred Scott, Carter Woodson, and Percy Julian—none of whose history was taught to me as a child. The conditioning was clear as day—the promoting of blacks as successful in the world of athletic abilities only. A world where the aggressiveness associated with our skin correlated to the violence of these respective sports. But it wasn't until I got older and thirsted to know my own history that these spearheading figures emerged from my research.

It taught me that as an African American boy, I was capable of more than just becoming a professional indentured servant on a multi-million dollar team. I learned other opportunities than just the NBA, NFL or MLB were out there for me. More importantly, I realized that the possibilities of becoming a renowned world leader representing an oppressed people were palpable. After obtaining this enlightenment, I also uncovered a new truth that America, *the land of the* un*free*, wasn't my greatest enemy; it was just a huge hurdle obstructing my course of self-identification.

I had to take a deeper look at where I would attribute blame for my constant shortcomings because it wasn't America nor the white privilege I once assumed it to be. It wasn't the institution of a single-parent home that I was raised in by my mother who had sacrificed everything she had to raise me. It wasn't my father whom I swore abandoned me with no lessons for how to circumvent this cycle of fatherless black sons. Neither of my parents failed me; it was I who ultimately failed them both. I was distracted by the conjecture of what was shown to me as a black youth.

For one to be born a black male in American society, it paints a horrible picture—a picture of anguish, a picture that illustrates inferiority. It depicts self-hatred and teaches us misconceptions about our own people.

The dried up blood spilled by black on black violence constructs the deep garnet brown pigment of our skin tone. The pitch-black ink of printed statistics that demonstrate the under-enrollment of African Americans in universities yet the overcrowding of blacks in prison yards fills the darkness within our pupils. While the burnt orange display of a prison jumpsuit fills-in the sun above, we look towards there for better days…but we know it will never come. The gray hues of black and white photos of Negroes swinging from trees like forbidden fruit are but outlines in the sky like wrinkles on our face. And the brown soil from the plantations on which our ancestors slaved covers us like a full head of hair. Like some traditional rites of passage, we wear these like tattoos.

Now let that picture resonate in your mind and ask yourself, "How can a black boy succeed when this picture is what he envisions himself to be?" As a member of generation Y millennials, I've seen the number of great leaders in the black community diminish tremendously. My generation is defined as people born between 1977–1994, those born in the era of the microwave and the age of the Internet. We are given flack for our loyalty to anything aside from our own personal desires and for being overly impatient—all things I can attest to.

Growing up I would hear of the struggles of our ancestors and of Civil Rights leaders who fought for our freedom. The likes of Rosa Parks not giving up her seat on the front of the bus where whites only were allowed to sit. Or Thurgood Marshall's incredible work on *Brown v. Board of Education*, desegregating schools in America. Or even someone like Ralph Abernathy Sr., co-founder of the Southern Christian Leadership Conference (SCLC), an organization formed by other pioneers of the movement like Bayard Rustin and Dr. Martin Luther King, Jr. Their sacrifices were courageous by all definitions, giving later generations a better chance at freedoms they themselves weren't granted access. These are rights that should be held to a higher degree and not taken for granted.

Yet to us, these are just stories of the past. We never witnessed the development of Dr. King's dream in the years following his death. We were born in a time when integration was expected, the norm. Interracial relationships and white and black kids sharing lunch tables were all we knew as a result of King's dream. We weren't recipients of the nightmarish ways of segregation in America, thus we have minimal appreciation.

Generation Y never felt the fire that pierced the heart of Detroit Red sparking a rebirth similar to that of the phoenix birthing Malcolm X. This transformation spawned from his appetite of knowledge and knowing the truth. Through the course of his life, he proved to be a fighter, combating the pitfalls of criminal ways, lack of education, and drug addictions. His hunger for knowledge never transferred over to us because we saw the results of possessing too much knowledge in America—death.

As a generation of technological advancement, we have yet to create a time machine that penetrates through the parallels of space, going back to learn what it means to lead people to a greater good. A greater good that cost most of our African American leaders their lives. The men of my generation were deprived of distinguished men to look up to in our community. Sadly, most of us never even knew what a man was until we turned on the television. We were born fatherless. Lost in society. We were taught it was normal for a black home to have an absent father.

> *"My father living in Memphis he can't come this way…boo hoo sad story, Black American Dad story,"*
> – Drake, a multiplatinum recording artist, describing the normality of having an absent father on his song, *Look What You've Done.*

We grew up without a man to teach us how to act accordingly.

How to make decisions with others in mind
How to treat a woman
How to stand with your chin held high against all odds

It ignites a spiteful passion in a boy to loathe his sperm donor. To hate the person you see in the mirror every day. The mirror reflecting the similarities between you and the person you vowed to be nothing like, your father. That man's face is just like yours, and nothing drives you madder than your mother's taunting, "You're just like your damn father." The greatest insult she or anyone else could ever say, scouring salt into an unhealed wound. You pray night and day to be everything your father wasn't. It becomes your greatest fear. The pressure of being the opposite of a great disappointment, with no blueprint of how to be better, becomes frustrating. You hate he will forever be a part of you. You hate you cannot know yourself or why you act in certain ways because you don't know him. You just hate. The sickness of hatred closes you off from feeling any other emotion.

You become ashamed of yourself, warding off any attempts to grow relationships. Any and everyone are subject to run off like he did. The fear of absenteeism breaks your fragile state of mind. People become revolving doors of missed opportunities. An absent father will cause more damage to his children than to the mother. A son begins to question if his mother can really teach him what it is to be a man. She can't. How could she possibly know what it takes to be man? A black man in America, *the land of the* un*free*, at that. Odds are she hasn't even seen a successful black man even to begin to base her parenting tactics on. And as a son, you don't even give her the credit she deserves for trying. You repay her with rebellious actions that belittle her authority and complicate the single-parent home even more.

You are left to the teachings of the world—teachings that can be counterproductive to a boy's development. You learn to take on more than your little shoulders can bear. You pick up the hardness of a man and become a ticking time bomb ready to spread pain. You become emotionless, lacking the ability to communicate feelings of what you are going through, crumbling all positive reinforcement previously received.

> *You build hatred.*
> *You build anger.*
> *You build frustration.*

Society shows us that a man shouldn't cry or feel anything. Teaching us that we, as men, should only be tough and strong. For a man is an extension of the gods and titans detailed in Greek mythology. Present-day warriors immune to all instances that provoke emotion. That seed of ignorance builds within until you realize just how wrong that truly is.

Time will go on and as you experience different situations, the growing pains will disrupt your common place of stability.

> *Why didn't he want to be my dad?*
> *Why didn't he at least love me enough to set aside his differences with my mom?*
> *Was it me that he didn't want?*
> *Maybe he was too much of a coward to raise me.*
> *As a matter of fact, f*ck him.*
> *I don't care because he's dead to me.*

The progression of thoughts running through your mind goes from sympathy to undaunted hate.

I can't be mad at him.
He made his choice.
It's going to be me and moms from here on out.
And best believe that once I make it, I won't have one inch of
forgiveness as he tries to claim me as his.
I got this on my own without anything from him.

You see, as you grow older, the possibilities for knowing yourself will be blocked by the discord between you and your father. How can you understand yourself without knowing both of the people who made you? At the end of it all, we are human beings who are the products of two parents and, through them, we learn so much about ourselves. The internal conflict forces you to consider making amends just so you can unlock the secrets of self. But remembering all the pain he caused halts you in your tracks. Keeping you in the dark from the truth.

Another pivotal aspect that will suffer is your love life. Love is one of the most complex mysteries of life but the absolute most necessary. It can cause you to feel so complete and fulfilled to the point where nothing else matters. But on the other hand, that same love can evolve into instant sickness once it is lost. Love is a mystery because no man ever actively demonstrated to you how to love unconditionally.

How to deal with heartbreaks?
How do you pick up the pieces and function without your loved
one?
When do you determine it's time to let go or keep fighting?
How can we begin to love someone else when we are not even
able to love ourselves?

Sure, our mothers can teach us how to be gentlemen. But in order to be a man, you must see a man. As a result, you leave behind a trail of tears from the hearts you've broken, as well as tears of your own. When you hurt someone you love, you end up truly hurting yourself even worse in the end. The long-term effect hangs over your head like it's overcast high in the sky. But once again you will hold it inside and feel too much pride to take responsibility for your actions. You don't bother to give that necessary effort required, demonstrating your love for a more than deserving young woman.

> *It seems as if nothing goes right.*
> *I'm pissed at the world.*
> *I can't keep a girl.*
> *Is my dad truly the blame for all this or am I?*
> *Am I really that bad of a person?*
> *I bust my ass every day to improve, but every day I get a door slammed in my face.*
> *Mom keep saying that God has something better for me but seems her prayers are falling upon the deaf ears of the Lord.*
> *Or is someone praying against me?*
> *No one can help me. No one can understand how I truly feel.*
> *This is my pain and I will own it!*
> *But when? When does it end? I know I'm strong, but I swear I can't take any more.*

The cauldron of pain, hurt, and anger boils into resentment in you. You become the blame for the shortcomings of your life and a punching bag for all of your problems. The weight of the world becomes too much, and you push away everyone who loves you.

Isolation befriends us.
Darkness consumes us.
Our mind becomes lost to the demons of our past.

A huge void will surface, and loneliness is the only feeling you will know. Waking up and looking in the mirror becomes the most difficult part of your day, realizing you have lost a different part of yourself. The mind is the most powerful aspect of a human, and you become overtaken by negative thoughts the more you ponder it. Questions of your worth will grow as rapidly as weeds in an unattended lawn. You doubt your purpose on this Earth and meaning to those around you because there is no self-love.

Just end it tonight; no one will miss you!

At that point, the conflict within you is near nuclear reaction. One side is telling you, *"You have so much to offer, so just believe."* The other side says, *"No one loves you, so just end your pain and take this NyQuil."*

As a black male who grew up with a single mother, I was that bastard child who hated the reflected image in the mirror. I can speak vividly to the feelings and consumption of negativity because I'm the product of these pains. The only way out for me was to suppress the bad memories in my mind and act as if they hadn't happened. But that was an unrealistic coping method that would prove to fail on several occasions. By age 18, I had experienced so many circumstances from which people don't recover and give in to the evils of their situations. In the end of it all, I contemplated suicide on several occasions.

As I got older and matured as a man, I began to realize I never properly dealt with the demons of my past. These unresolved issues would impact every decision I made moving forward. Some of these decisions determined my path while others would destroy any happiness I could grasp onto.

> *I stopped blaming others for my problems.*
> *I realized my pain was self-inflicted.*
> *I was my own worst enemy.*

My selfishness and unstableness as a man became so immense that I would break down crying in public and wouldn't know why. I robbed my loved ones of the liveliness I had inside because I was so full of pain from years of holding it in. Love did not abide within me, and I was ashamed. I was so infatuated with being everything my father wasn't that I became a hypocrite. The similarities were so obvious that even a blind man could see them. It wasn't until I lost everything that I was able to fix the broken image of myself.

> *I was human.*
> *I was imperfect.*

I was ready to accept those facts because the way I was viewing myself for years was going to force me only into further depression and darkness. The hate I had within had to die—not only for my sake, but also for the people who grew up experiencing the same obstacles that I had. I want to let them know it is not the end. You can forgive yourself and you can grow.

> *Forgiveness is the first step in conquering your enemy.*
> *After that comes understanding.*
> *Followed by love.*

As I found myself in a place of solitude, away from any distractions or further masking of my deeper issues through unhealthy relationships, I was able to address my excuses for my selfishness and shortcomings. After 24 years, I looked at myself in mirrors. And do you know what I saw in those reflections? An empty, disfigured shape, lifeless on the inside, screaming for help from behind prison bars of pitiful pride and fathomless fear. These mirrors reflected every monster embedded deep within my molecular makeup, which I suppressed in memory or tried to outrun…

"Run…run…just run," was an echoing phrase that kept me away from helping myself. I was so lost in my mess that I couldn't decipher the difference between joy and depressed, suicidal thoughts. These mirrors became the gateway to self-forgiving freedom— freedom from carrying things I should have left in my childhood, blame I credited to other people, and even assassination attempts I planned on myself.

As your own worst enemy, the battle is everlasting until you can forgive yourself, understand the reasoning behind your unwise choices, and learn to love yourself no matter what. Only then can you stop asking, "Who is the enemy?"

T.H.U.G. L.I.F.E.

THE ENEMY: *You're destined to lose. People don't care anything about you. You can't beat the odds, you're no anomaly, and you're just like the other failures known as black men. Born to lose and built to succumb to your surroundings.*

"THUG LIFE MUTHAFUCKA! THAT'S ALL I GOT TO SAY, THUG LIFE. I'll die screaming it until they bury a G. Y'all will never understand," words from the late great Tupac Amaru Shakur. By profession, he was a successful rapper and actor . By his gift, he was the blunt voice of the reality of an oppressed people. Outspoken and educated with the ear of the people, Tupac had an army of listeners eager to follow his new black movement. His platform put him at the forefront of racial tensions when the misrepresentations of blacks continued in America from the very first time he uttered, "Thug Life."

According to Merriam-Webster, a "thug" is defined as *a violent criminal; a brutal ruffian or assassin.* The word "life" is denoted as *the ability to grow, change, etc.*[1] by combining these definitions, therefore, one would think "Thug Life" meant *possessing the aptitude to demonstrate change and growth over time as a violent offender*. However, according to Tupac, its true meaning is broken down as The Hate You Gave Little Infants F*cks Everybody. The acronym THUG LIFE served as a powerful phrase that represented the reciprocation of minorities exposed to unfit educational systems, poorer living conditions, higher unemployment rates—surrounded by meritocracy.

> "When I say Thug Life, I mean that shit cause these white folks see us as thugs, I don't care what ya'll think. I don't care if you think you're a lawyer, if you a man, if you an African American. If you whatever the fuck you think you are. We thugs and niggers to these motherfuckers. And until we own some shit, Imma call it like it is. How you gone be a man and we starving? You know. And you walk by five different houses and ain't a man in either one of them motherfuckers. How we gone be a man? How we gone be African Americans, we out here dying? We thugs and we niggers until we set this shit right. Trust me when I say that shit."[2]

Tupac's Thug Life was a new black movement charged to undermine the misconceptions of black males and others whom he deemed underdogs in America. He charged us to take responsibility for our actions, exemplifying what it means to be a *two-fisted thoroughbred man*. One who stands for more than the values of his homeboys but for the advancement of his community. A fighter, not of the knuckles, of the mind that liberates him of the preconceptions fed to him since birth. A man free of the pressure of being "black enough," one comfortable in his own skin amongst those who look like him, especially in front of those who do not. The questioning of one's authenticity spawns an inescapable anxiety.

As a people with no true understanding of our ancestral roots, aside from what European colonialism has to say on the subject and with not one history book to teach us of our significance, finding ourselves has been a strenuous process. The twoness of the term African-American as described by W. E .B. Du Bois are combating factions.

> [A]n American, a Negro; two souls, two thoughts two unreconciled strivings; two warring ideals in one dark body, whose dogged strength alone keeps it from being torn asunder.

> The history of the American Negro is the history of this strife, - this longing to attain self-conscious manhood, to merge his double self into a better and truer self. In this merging he wishes neither of the older selves to be lost. He would not Africanize America, for America has too much to teach the world and Africa. He would not bleach his Negro soul in a flood of white Americanism, for he knows that Negro blood has a message for the world. He simply wishes to make it possible for a man to be both a Negro and an American, without being cursed and spit upon by his fellows, without having the doors of Opportunity closed roughly in his face.[3]

This same process of self-discovery has been met with opposition from within and outside of our community. Internally, one hears statements like, "You talk white" when demonstrating one's command of the English language, and "You actin' white" when attempting to fit in with the majority. Outside our community, our every move is criticized and viewed with a judging eye. Walking down the street amongst whites, as a black man, you're likely to see them clutch their belongings tighter, lock their doors immediately behind them, or do any and everything possible to avoid you. Self-worth—what is it when acceptance doesn't come from those who can relate to you or from those who have oppressed you according to the standards of history?

Elaborating more on the intended meaning of Tupac's Thug Life—young black males who were on the receiving end of disadvantaged circumstances would then exhale all the poison they inhaled back into society. For me, Thug Life was a mindset I adopted from my very first conscious thought since birth, consuming every wrongdoing of family members, friends, naysayers and from whomever didn't believe my life was worth living.

"I recommend abortion. If you go through with this pregnancy, your child will be born with spinal bifida and will depend on the two of you for the duration of his life," the doctor told my parents, a 23-year-old Toni Williamson and 20-year-old Larry Brown, Jr. "If he beats the odds, he'll be lucky to live six months. Past that, he will be bound to a wheelchair. The two of you are young. I just see how this can be a huge strain on young parents. You can always try again, but the decision is yours," the doctor concluded. The impact of such explosive news was enough to level a small country. They were new to the whole idea of having a child, so I was a blessing to their lives, and no one wants to accept the fact that their child could be here and gone within a matter of months. The pressure mounted as the delivery due date neared.

My mother was the recipient of the devil's persuasive power to manipulate the mind to work against one's faith. During her pregnancy, she suffered from severe posttraumatic stress disorder (PTSD). She had been laid off from her job at Green Shield & Purple Cross when she was seven months pregnant. Now the idea of losing her son crippled her faith in everything, including herself.

> I can remember when the doctor and the nurse came into the room. It was cold enough that I quivered; I was in a lot of pain and stressed out. I was anxious and bottling up too many emotions. I

didn't even feel prepared to have a child. The doctor told us it would be best if I had an abortion. And at one point I contemplated doing so. I didn't have a job or any means to take care of myself let alone a child. And I'm looking at Ismael's father questioning if he was ready because he was much younger than I was.

I can remember the emptiness from within and how this would leave an everlasting scar on my heart. "If you decide to have this child, he'll never walk and the two of you will have to take care of him the rest of his life." Just echoed in the back of my mind.

I looked over at Larry as the news sunk in and I could see the disinterest all over his face. We were both young and had so much to live for. But one thing was for certain, Ismael was one of those things. I trusted God and knew he was the giver of life and not death. For it was not in his plan to abort this gift he had given us.

Just five years prior to my birth, my mom had lost her mother to colon cancer, and she doubted her own abilities to be a mother. She didn't have anyone to rely on, reliving the fact that she was motherless. My grandfather, her father, was a man of many children, but he wasn't much of a parent to any of them. So my mother was left to learn how to parent on her own, and it scared the hell out of her. She became angry knowing she had no positive male figure for me to learn lessons of life from. The fear of failing as a parent and the fact that I could be afflicted with a terminal illness sent her into a deep depression.

I would cry for hours. I trusted God but this was a true test of my faith. The doctors had prescribed for me anti-depressants, but I wasn't sold on taking them. I really didn't want to become dependent on them.

In contrast, my father grew up in a solid home with a great foundation. A military brat, who was born in Ludwigsburg, Germany, to Larry Brown, Sr. and Hattie Mae Brown in June 1970. My father grew up a happy kid, blessed enough to see the world at an early age. The foundational base was there for him to rely upon when he had children one day. For him the dilemma of potentially aborting me or having a sick child came from the absence of light.

> This was my first-born son, the one who would carry my family name. There was no way in fuckin' hell I was going to abort him. But it began to eat at me, to see how everything affected Toni. Unlike me, she was so deep-rooted in her faith and to witness how broken she was, it really hit me. It ripped me up inside! Like what did I do to deserve this? But I knew Ismael was going to see the light of this world, and we would figure out everything else that came with his birth.

But my father became a true product of his environment. My grandfather was a humble, sweet man—with a vice that would ultimately end his life. He was an alcoholic, and this was a path my father also walked on. For my dad, life's punches and blows would soften by the time he reached the bottom of a liquor bottle. It was history repeating itself all over again, like father like son. Aged 19 when I was conceived, my father was living a life of the young and lost. He ran with a much older crowd, often indulging in the same debaucheries as they did. But how could any difference be expected when that's what he grew up around and still encompassed him?

My parents gave me a true understanding of the phrase "opposites attract." They came from different worlds and upbringings.

They met each other in 1988 at Green Shield & Purple Cross where they worked. My mom was a claims examiner and was responsible for reviewing all types of medical cases, abiding by contractual agreements and benefit plans. My father was a customer service representative, screening calls from customers with questions and concerns, providing quality assurance.

The decision was made to proceed with my birth. I came into the world on Sunday, October 28, 1990. I was taken home a few days later—completely spinal bifida free. However, I wasn't completely free of disabilities. In the following months, I would return to the doctor for walking braces on my legs and feet. For once, it appeared my doctors actually knew what they were talking about. I developed clubfeet—the heels of my feet touched each other, interfering with the functionality of my lower limbs. I was a young Forest Gump well before the movie released in 1994. After receiving these walking braces at the age of four months, it wouldn't take much time to begin proving why I was special. By eight and one-half months, I simply began walking, completely skipping the crawling stage. "Ismael didn't crawl. It was amazing. Before you knew it, he began running everywhere. I couldn't let him out of my sight because he was bound to fall immediately. His little body couldn't keep up with his realigned feet and that big ole head of his," my mom recalled laughingly.

The leap of faith my parents took was beginning to show significant signs of life. Because of these early childhood events, I've always managed to disregard the likes of a doctor's prognosis. When God's the ultimate healer and creator, what value do man's words truly have? I will never forget that doctor's expert recommendation to abort me. It became a reminder I wasn't supposed to be here. A reminder that discharged a deep passion down in my soul to justify I had a purpose for my life. All I had to do was discover what it was.

Not too much later after I was born, my parents went their separate ways. Both of them were young and still searching for not only self-fulfillment but also themselves. Their shared love for me was the only thing that kept them in contact with each other.

Age five is as far back as I can remember. Back then my mother proved to be a woman of extraordinary abilities. Having parted ways with my father and being parentless, her survival skills kicked into high gear. We bounced around from one apartment complex to the next and relied heavily on public transportation, all while she searched for a stable career. What impressed me most about catching three buses in the rain just to get groceries was she never complained. Not once. I admired her abilities to withstand and keep going. I wanted nothing more than to embody the same skill of resilience.

> I had to fight for my child. If I didn't, then who else would? Each other, that's all we had. But I didn't have the time to feel sorry for myself. I had a mouth to feed. My faith kept me going, knowing I had a responsibility greater than myself. Was I scared? Yes, what 24-year-old young woman wouldn't be? But I couldn't sit around waiting for something to happen or worrying about what the absent parent wasn't doing. I had to do my part as a parent.

By the time I turned six, my mom had secured a new job that showed promise for long-term employment. The job ultimately materialized into a career. Her new role required a great deal of expertise and self-awareness. She was now responsible for overseeing the condemned individuals of society who required rehabilitation at the cost of tax-payer dollars. She would now be known as Correctional Officer T.D. Williamson. As the rookie on her squad, she was given what THE DEPUTY'S OFFICE considered the "graveyard" shift, working from 11pm to 7am. Her correctional duties consisted of supervising inmates in housing units and prisoners separated for administrative or punitive purposes. In addition, duties included creating a safe environment that included surprise periodic patrols of housing units, booking new inmates, and establishing the rules of their new surroundings of forfeited freedom.

This opportunity was granted to my mother upon completion of the police academy, which challenged her mentally, physically, and emotionally. The academy wasn't about how fast or far you could run, since the physical build of correctional officers was only half that required of police officers. The mental cost was more than demanding—dealing with people who were blackballed by society because of one mistake and repeat offenders who couldn't find a better lifestyle. The clash of such personalities and combative souls rebelling against natural order can break anyone. Emotionally, you're dealing with setting aside your moral compass, judgment, and any remorse felt towards an inmate. The academy touched you on each level in a tri-fold haze.

When my mother worked the night shift, I didn't have a babysitter, nor did I go to my father's house. I was home alone, responsible for myself. She made sure we ate dinner together and spent quality time before leaving. In no form or fashion did I smite or chide her for leaving me alone. At six, what I knew was mommy had to provide for us and if that equated to me being alone at night, then so be it. After I got over the fear of being alone, I began to actually enjoy it. I was free to stay up as late as I wanted, watch whatever scary movie was on late night TV, and could eat all the junk food in the house. Not all fun and games, the companionless time also forced me to mature faster than I should have. Through this unattended time, the introvert in me was born. I learned to fend for myself in the forms of ensuring the house was clean before my mom got home from work to being on alert for intruders. *Responsibility* was a word I valued and took more seriously than the norms of being the child I was. The essence of a childhood was no more.

My mother spoke to me like an adult, creating expectations of competency and reciprocation. She was conscious that help wasn't coming in the form of a man raising me, so she did what she felt was necessary. She hid nothing from me, thoroughly explaining the depths of growing up in a world where the cards were stacked against me and having to take ownership of my life. Not once did I ever want to disappoint her, so I challenged myself to raise my level of maturity, even though I didn't know how. I would do everything I could to comprehend the messages she delivered. I began mimicking what I thought were adult ways by watching her. My mother continued to drill in me that the cards were stacked against me simply because I was a black fatherless boy. "Son, society has already counted you out. You must be smarter than they think you are. Education is key. That's one thing no one can ever take away from you." We spent a considerable amount of time together, subsiding any chances that I would fall victim to the streets. The streets that built an institution always at the ready, enrolling new foot soldiers to stand toe to toe against opposition, given no rules of engagement only weapons of self-destruction—cocaine, weed, pills and guns. The recruiting methods weren't spectacular, but the positioning and availability was by far superior to any of the other institutions like schools, churches, or the home. My mother fully understood the dynamics of how black males fall shameless victims to the streets from watching her younger brother, Magic, and working at a correctional facility.

She understood she had to keep me busy and on a consistent schedule, so I wouldn't wander out into the concrete jungle. As a single mother and lover of sports, she decided to sign me up for a couple programs. In my younger years, I played football under the moniker *Happymeal*, being the obese kid who barely made weight on game days. I wasn't half bad playing offensive guard, though I was better at linebacker on defense. I wore the number 40 for the Woodland Acre Wolverines in the Boys and Girls Club League. Mom never missed a game, not one. Still working the night shift, she remained committed to supporting her son.

Because I put my mom on a high pedestal, I took her every word for gold. I vowed to achieve what no one could ever take from me, my education. My focus abandoned childish ways and locked on ways to beat the odds. I became an avid reader, absorbing any and every book in sight. I stopped going outside, interacting with kids in my apartment complex, and began closing out all other kid-approved activities. "Boop, you must out work all the kids in your class," Mom would say. All her lessons became new goals I had to achieve. Failing my mother wasn't an option. She was very active in my academic success, establishing rapport with each of my elementary school teachers, assuring them that they had her support at home. They formed a team, enriching me with constant feedback and positive assurance when completing schoolwork. It was clear that being a subpar student wasn't acceptable in my household.

I was a witness to all her sacrifices for me; the least I could do was to put some effort into my part. In school I became the model academic student, fearless in overachieving. I possessed all the qualities of a child prodigy with one major flaw—my attitude. I grew up in a single-parent home that offered no sugarcoating, blunt honesty only. I became an instant reflection of my teachings outside of the home. In school I was a brilliant agitator, creating dissonance across the classroom.

My conduct in elementary school was far from desirable. My acting out was an embarrassment. I went to school, finished my work, and then transformed into the troublemaker every teacher dreaded. "Ismael, go flip your card right now," my second-grade teacher, Mrs. Johnson, would demand. But little did she know—I didn't care anything about flipping some stupid card from an A to a B. In my mind, as along as it wasn't an F, I had more free passes to do as I pleased. I couldn't understand why she was so angry with me. All my schoolwork was completed and done right. I was a daily terror as soon as I stepped out of my mom's aqua-green Subaru Impreza onto the campus of Lone Star Elementary on the southside of Jacksonville, Florida.

Every day my mom took me to school after working all night long. She drove 30 minutes to pick me up at home and another 30 minutes to drop me off at school. She was beyond exhausted, but she did it with a smile on her face. "Have a good day, Boop. I love you," she said, kissing me goodbye. And I repaid her efforts with multiple calls home from fed up teachers who were done dealing with a disrespectful child, unwilling to conform to the norms of classroom behavior. The decline in my respect for authority and the institution of school took a drastic turn in the 2nd grade.

"It's show and tell time, guys! If everyone could come sit in a circle, Indian style, as we get ready to share our cool experiences with one another. Who wants to go first?" My 2nd grade teacher instructed and asked.

This was an activity I couldn't care less for. I really didn't see the point of exploiting one another's financial backgrounds. Especially as a kid, I felt embarrassed when kids of wealthier families brought the newest toys their parents bought them. It burned away at my soul. *"Why can't I have something cool to show?"* It taught me nothing about education but everything about life. People praise the haves and shun the have nots who place survival above all.

Usually, I was good about hiding my dislike for this pointless activity, but I was barring a secret that made hiding emotion almost impossible. So this time, show and tell was different. My secret made me scold the brats and everything they had.

Who cares you got WWE Smackdown on Sony Playstation?
You're still dumb. My grades are way better than yours.
You can't even bring that in to show, dummy.
You could be lying for all we know.

"Okay, it's your turn," Mrs. Johnson said to the kid next to me. He, unlike me, never had an issue expressing his acrimony for show and tell; he commonly passed and ignored all the other kids. When it came time to pass around the newest action figures or hair clips, he wouldn't even flinch at admiring them. He was totally unresponsive. But today was different for him, too. His eyes were as empty as the stomach of a famished child in a 3rd world country, his clothes reeked of yesterday's lunch, dirt stains all over his shirt.

> *Man, someone get this guy a hot bath and some soap;*
> *he smells like hot trash juice.*
> *How could he come to school like this?*
> *Where are his parents?*
> *Do they not care about him?*
> *Man, he stinks!*

His body tensed up as Mrs. Johnson asked again. He stared in a daze in the middle of nowhere and finally said, "You know I don't have anything to show, but I do have something to tell…I wish I was dead. I'm tired of walking the streets all night with holes in my shoes and hearing my little brother cry from being so tired. If I were dead, I wouldn't have to come here and hide from all you ungrateful punks, pretending you were my friends."

He revealed he was homeless. It became too much to hold inside. While I was complaining to myself and being a vanity slave—he and I could actually relate. I can remember Mrs. Johnson's facial expression to this day; she looked like a failed teacher, mother, and even as a human being. As she fought back tears, she got up immediately to end our weekly show and tell session—for the rest of the school year. "Come with me." They walked outside together, and that would be the last chance I ever got to talk to someone who knew what I was going through. I was homeless, too. Just too afraid to speak up and speak out. Too fearful of the consequences that could be levied by child services. Too prideful to exemplify pain or weakness because boys didn't do that.

As I grew older and social media came to the forefront of pop culture, I looked him up on various sites. Every single year I searched his name, looking for some type of indication he was still… alive. I never told anyone this story but felt it was important I find him to see how he was doing. It was sad to see just how devastated he was emotionally. For him, life wasn't worth living and by the age of eight, he was already defeated.

As a hardheaded, resentful seven-year-old, soon to be eight, I discovered school was more than a place of learning; it became my playground for mischievous behavior, spawning from the fear of the unknown. You see, unlike most other kids, I didn't know what awaited me on the other side of that 3pm school bell. I was given the real world at an early age, and it created a cold little boy, enraged at situations he could not understand, ready to inflict his pain on anyone in sight.

I drove Mrs. Johnson crazy. She was an older lady nearing retirement who truly loved her craft of teaching. It gave her a sense of responsibility in molding the future, but I looted her joy without any regret. Mrs. Johnson's daily excitement began to sizzle with the constant battles and exchanges of words with a troubled child. "Ismael, do you want another referral?"

"I don't care, Mrs. Johnson," I responded. My frustration with Mrs. Johnson grew because I was demanding help through my actions, but she never acknowledged more was going on in me than just trouble in school. I felt she failed me as a caring educator. Not once did she pull me to the side to get to the bottom of my behavioral issues. She dismissed my cries for help, just applying a Band-Aid to her problem by giving me referral after referral. I simply wanted her to try. Would I have told her what was really going on? Probably not, but knowing she cared, I maybe would have contemplated going a little bit easier on her.

By age eight, my life had become an enigma. My grandfather was diagnosed with cirrhosis, which savagely progressed into cancer of the liver from years of alcohol abuse. It was evident all his drinking had caught up to him, ready to claim his life. Simultaneously, my mother had just given birth to my sister, and we were homeless. Yet I still had to go to school, be studious and respectful—an Oscar award-winning actor who played the role of the happiest kid in America.

Guess no one cares what I'm going through.
My sister will be born in all this mess, and there's nothing I can do.

My beloved baby sister was born on Sunday, December 28, 1997. Monica Rae weighed 4lbs 11oz and was two months too early. She was so frail and tiny the doctors demanded she remain under their surveillance for a few more weeks. I viewed it as God's way of protecting her from the hell that mom and I were firmly standing in. The epidemic of homelessness was something I'd never thought I would experience. I assumed people were homeless because of sheer laziness. What did I know about the hardships facing adults? Who the hell did I think I was to judge? But I would soon find out just how hard it was to be nomadic.

Mom and I bounced between two hotels located off University Blvd., not too far from Englewood High School and University Christian Academy. One of the hotels was a Days Inn, the other a Ramada Inn. They were directly across the street from each other. Before then, I'd never seen the inside a hotel, let alone slept in one for weeks at a time. They weren't your five-star room service hotels, but they weren't your roach infested motels either.

The Days Inn room we lived in was relatively small with dimmed lighting and a barely functioning television set. We unloaded all our things we had packed down into my mom's car and made the Days Inn "home." The room had one queen size bed we both slept in. I wondered how many people before us had shared this same bed for God only knows what type of adventures, or how many families had been in our very identical predicament. But, nonetheless, we were here, and this was our reality. We had no kitchen in which to cook, so we ate out nightly, feasting on the best of University Blvd.'s fast-food offerings. I was just glad to have a full stomach more than anything. I would lie there at night, dreaming of the day we could leave this place and have our own.

> *I can't wait until this is over.*
> *I'll never step foot inside a hotel ever again.*
> *I just wish I was be able to fix this.*
> *There's nothing I can do; I'm too young.*
> *I'm nothing but a mouth to feed.*
> *But I have to be strong for Mom, no tears or complaining.*

My mom continued to exercise her more than superhero abilities by not showing any signs of grief or remorse for our situation. We never talked about it or waddled in self-pity. We both continued with our day to day as if this situation were normal. She showed me how to remain steadfast in the face of adversity. A lesson I took to heart and clinched tightly because it was a prequel for what life would later have for me.

The only time I was able to escape this place was at school or at the hospital visiting my sister—the new light of my world, giving me so much to live for. I wanted nothing more than to be the perfect big brother. The one who showed her how to ride a bike, her protector against older kids picking on her, and ready to interrogate all dudes wanting a piece of her heart. Not only would I have someone to play with, I also had someone looking up to me, so I would have to be conscious of my actions moving forward. I charged myself with being the precedent she would follow, creating a positive role model.

While at the hospital, I heard awful stories of how older siblings were destined to envy the newest addition to the family. But I couldn't fathom being jealous of someone so beautiful. I just feared failing her as an older brother, not being able to be there to fight every battle for her or protect her from every knee scrape. When she was released from the hospital, it was a bittersweet moment. "She's cleared to go home," the doctor said, but I remembered the word "home" didn't have much relevance to us because we didn't have one.

By this time we had moved into the Ramada Inn. An upgrade from the previous setup we had at the Days Inn just days ago; we now had two twin-size beds. My sister was here now, and it dawned on me how fortunate she was to be so young that she would never remember these times. I never saw the need to remind her of the gloomy times, spawning questions her young mind couldn't process or causing her to become angry with absent family members, holding a crippling grudge against them. But we were just like any other family. We were not perfect and had a multitude of issues that boiled over to the point of heated arguments, fights, and regrettable phrases like *"get out of my house."*

With nowhere else to go, how could a family member knowingly tell my mom, a small child, and a newborn to *get out of my house*? But we were family, right? And loved one another, right? Where was the love when our clothes and toys started flying out the front door onto the front yard? Where was the love when tear ducts flooded my mother's eyes as she picked up our belongings from the lawn? Why wasn't love stronger than pride? Why couldn't love overpower disagreement? How could no one see what this was doing to me? Guess the blood we shared wasn't thick enough, and love wasn't real. This defining moment would prove to be the root of my distrust for all people. My whole outlook on life was shaken because if family could inflict this type of agony on a child, then a stranger wouldn't think twice about killing me. Everyone in sight became the opposition.

Growing older with that type of perspective and absolute mindset, anyone attempting to get close to me possessed an ulterior motive and was out to get me. Limited in my understanding, I assumed I had a quality they wanted to take advantage of, or I had access to things or people they desired. No one received the benefit of the doubt; my heart and mind formed an impenetrable blockade, keeping everyone out, even my mother. *Never again will someone betray me like that.* The people who scared me most were the ones who professed their love for me. That word carried significant weight and responsibility. Love was the foundation for kinship, trust, openness and vulnerability. *Love* is categorized as a noun, but in its truest form, it involves action. Therefore, it is a verb. It can be a full-time job attempting to love someone.

Expressing love required a profound connection with another individual that tied together both people emotionally. One's love for another evolves over time and plants itself in a person's core, becoming a part of who one is. But over time and through many experiences with family members and others in relationships ranging in dynamics, whether friends or girlfriends, showed me that the people whom you love have the greatest power over your emotions and thoughts. Therefore, love equips them with all the ammunition needed to destroy you. I learned there truly is a thin line between love and hate, stemming from a turn of events between two compassionate individuals. The mass accumulation of feelings can warp from uplifting joy to drowning disparity without a life jacket.

I didn't want to be loved, truthfully. I couldn't bear another traumatic experience with a loved one. I figured it was safer this way; it was my personal defense mechanism. Keeping people out saved us both any potential hardships. As time went by in my life, it became harder for me to formulate relationships and true connections with family—and people in general. By failing to establish sustainable connections, I pushed a great deal of people away. I prejudged them on the potential damage they could do to me; the logic was poor and had very little validity. Instead of informing these people of my concerns and communicating effectively, I passed on these opportunities numerous times to open up when I really needed to purge myself of my ignorant mindset. Optically, everyone was capable of evil, and forgiveness didn't reside in my heart. Realistically, this way of thinking removed me from experiencing the life lessons one can only learn from interactions with people. A piece of self can be discovered through one's willingness to add value to a relationship's dynamic. With family, ideally, the love you have allows you to be there for them in times of need and to the degree you are comfortable in sacrificing yourself for their betterment. I felt like an outsider in my own family. My thoughts, drive, and compassion were just so different than those of my family. I kept my views to myself, fearful of conflict or offending anyone. I truly felt like an alien at times. In dating, love matures from what's best for me to what's best for us, from I to we. Once again self becomes a secondary concern. Without these attempts at love, I never learned to be selfless in my relationships. Introspectively, not once did I ask God for clarity or direction. My faith wasn't that strong, but my disdain for people was. God was love; therefore, I denounced him continuously.

My next tragedy came just months later—on January 15, 1998 to be exact—when the angel of death entered the VA hospital of Gainesville. He causally walked the chilly and drab hallways undetected. Clothed in all black garments that draped to the floor, his face was covered by a free forming hood. There was no identifying this ominous figure by any name other than *death*. Gliding across the floors in lament, he passed room after room, visually capturing families exhibiting cheerful spirits in the hopes their loved ones would at some point walk out of this morbid place. He continued on collecting the souls of those God commanded him to retrieve. Unfortunately, on that day, he entered my Papa's room, where my dad, Granny, aunt and other relatives stood by his bedside. Without warning, death took him, just one day after doctors professed my grandfather was doing better than they had ever seen him do. And just like that, he left me. Didn't even say, "Goodbye, Rocket." He just gave up the fight.

> *How could you leave me?*
> *I need you, Papa.*
> *Who's going to teach me how to fish now?*
> *Papa, what am I going to do without you?*
> *All I wanted to do was see you one last time.*
> *I can't…*

I remember the last thing Papa said to me: "Rocket, you take care of your little sister and your mom." He knew his time was nearing. I never forgot his last words, and I swore to do as he had instructed.

For years following his death, I felt as if he had a choice in all of this and decided to leave me behind. I selfishly blamed his death on him as if he wanted to die. I was too young to understand it was his time to meet his maker and would be free of pain in Heaven next to his Father. The one thought that engulfed my mind was that I was stuck here without him. I ignored the pain he was experiencing from the chemotherapy and the relentless pain that drinking left him with. Back then my pain superseded his. It was all about my own personal needs. I didn't know any better and searched for years to find ways to forgive my self-centered ways.

My grandfather and I were inseparable, and the whole family knew it. He called me Rocket, his go to man. We had shared so many unforgettable experiences, from chasing chickens for dinner to watching the Atlanta Braves with Grandma Elaine during the young

Chipper Jones days. After Papa's military days, he was a cashier at the local Winn-Dixie in Callahan, Florida, and people loved him. Big Larry, as he was known, was a town favorite; everyone wanted to be in is check-out lane. He was full of personality, humor, and joy. I can remember him bringing me yellow powdered Gatorade and specially preparing a glass for me. I always asked how he made it because mine never tasted the same as his. He knew how to keep young Rocket intrigued and elated.

Papa and I had built an unbreakable bond. During these times, nothing made my father happier than knowing his son could receive the same love he did growing up. The Brown family name had never been stronger than when my grandfather was alive. It wasn't until his departure from this earth that the foundation gave way.

From what I remember of his funeral, the church didn't have one empty seat, standing room only. The sanctuary was filled with family, friends, locals who knew the family, and military veterans who'd served with my grandfather in the Army. I can recall riding to the church in the family limo, peeking out the window, seeing how much of an impact he had on the Callahan community. His peers cherished him, and it made me proud to be his Rocket. Before exiting the limo, I remember how quiet my dad was during the ride from my great grandmother's house to the church. My father's joking nature was obsolete, not a cracking smile in sight. I found myself mimicking his ability to demonstrate a lack of outward expression, but soon I would be the only one not showing any sadness. Sitting in that church and looking at everyone so distraught was overwhelming. No one around me could remain emotionally stable. One of my grandfather's best friends, whose name I cannot extract from memory, recollected over the microphone the good times they had together. Then hysteria crushed him. It was my first time seeing a man that broken over anything or anyone. I felt bad not being able to cry. I didn't want anyone to think I loved him any less than they did. But had they grown up with me in the coming years, they would have counted the tears, multiplied by 10, that fell night after night well into my adulthood. They would know exactly how much he meant to me.

Losing my grandfather was a daily battle, waking up every morning knowing he was no longer there for me. I was living in a barren land—free of vegetation and in severe drought. My hunger for the wisdom my Papa could have bestowed upon me coupled with my thirst to have him by my side each day decimated me. When I was in high school, I asked Granny for a picture of him, and she was generous enough to give me several. It was difficult to ask for fear of evoking memories about my Papa because I didn't know how she would feel parting ways with the photos or where she was in her healing process. The pictures she gave me were of the days when he was in the service, and he never looked better. One was a black and white 5" x 7" photo that showed him posing with a propped up leg and leaning over in a relaxed pose. It captured his personality—an easygoing man who enjoyed the thrills and chills of life, a simple man who did not want much but possessed it all in spirit. In contrast, the second picture, a framed 8" x 10" color headshot of him in uniform, captured the softer side of Papa. He was the most giving human being I'd ever encountered, even to this day. This was an attribute I knew I wasn't capable of having, but I wanted to mirror the prestigious man I remembered him to be.

After his passing, visits to Callahan didn't make sense to me anymore. I had no one with whom to run around the big dirt-filled yard, no one to talk about old war stories and, more importantly, no one to call me Rocket. The closest person I had to my Papa on this Earth was his younger brother, Johnny Brown. To be honest, it frightened me to be round him. The older my uncle Johnny grew, the more he looked like my Papa—from their strong build to their thick, smoky grey and black mustache, down to the identical flattop haircut they sported. My uncle Johnny also referred to me as Rocket, but it burned my ears to hear that name. *Only my Papa can call me that. He's dead and so is that name.* I never wanted to go back to Callahan; the whole town was just a reminder of what I'd lost.

My father, on the other hand, had other plans for me. I cringed at the thought of going back; it caused a tightening in my chest, shortness of breath, and a sharp pain deep in my abdomen. I recall pouting immediately after my father suggested the idea. Being so young and unable to effectively communicate, I did not once think to tell my dad why I didn't want to go. But as an adult, he knew the importance of cultivating relationships with the rest of the family still in Callahan, and that's all he wanted for his son. My youthful thinking couldn't reach the capacity of his thinking. To be honest, at the time, I didn't care. A part of me blamed the family for allowing my Papa to drink freely. I always questioned in my mind what if someone had tried to stop him, warn him of the damage he was inflicting upon himself, let alone those who cherished him? Seemed to me everyone just turned a blind eye to the severity of his condition as an alcoholic. I felt my family enabled my Papa's condition by condoning the drinking.

> *Papa would still be alive if you just stopped him, Granny.*
> *Uncle Johnny, why didn't you get your brother some help?*
> *Now he's gone and all we have to hold are fading memories.*
> *Now I have to grow up without him.*

I did not know much about alcoholism, nor the commanding hold it can have on its victims. Such an illness creates a sense of dependency, alters your day-to-day activities, and can cause you to lash out on everyone around you. The sickness becomes a part of who you are. Papa was a functioning alcoholic, so he was able to maintain his daily activities. Such an illness can alter your thoughts and create a sense of dependency on alcohol. I just wanted to know from what he was running, or what was he trying to suppress? Was his life really that hard? I really didn't know, nor did I ever get the chance to ask him. Maybe he needed to talk through some of the issues that troubled him. My list of questions grew endlessly with no answers coming.

Everything my dad knew was in Callahan. Even as a military child who had lived abroad and was cultured by the age of 12, he was your everyday country boy who thrived in the elements of the back-woods. By the time my father was in high school, he and my uncle Jacob went to live with their grandmother, my great-grandmother Elaine. All of his high school friends, older cousins, and life lessons were products of Callahan; he refused to part ways with them all.

I remember back to the times we visited Callahan before the passing of my Papa. I saw the glow in his eyes, knowing he was taking me back to his roots. My father loved the change of pace, going back and forth from the city to the country. It gave him a sense of appreciation for his upbringing. It was therapeutic. I noticed how at ease he was around my great-grandmother and how he outwardly expressed his love for her and the sacrifice she made in raising him. Being with my dad in Callahan was like being with a celebrity returning home. All I heard was, "Lil Larry, is that you?" Everyone in Callahan knew him as "Lil Larry" and became overly excited when they saw him. "Lil Larry, you look good man. How's your grandma? I've been meaning to go see her." Literally, every single person we encountered would comment and inquire about my great-grandmother. She was a staple in the Callahan community. She was responsible for raising many kids who either had parents of their own or who would have been victims of child services if she hadn't volunteered to care for them. It was times like these that I thought the world of my father. However, things drastically changed between my father and me as a result of the death of Papa.

My adolescent years would continue with everyday issues most young boys faced. I grew more eager to reach adulthood, challenged my mother in ways that disrespected her authority, and thought I knew it all. My mother tried everything she could to "raise a man," but we both knew it wasn't possible. On several occasions, my disrespect concluded in me being thrown out of the house. I just didn't listen. She would ask me to do simple things like wash the dishes, fold the clothes she had washed, clean meat for dinner, or mop the floor. Simple things. But at times, I didn't see the need in me doing so. I felt those chores were womanly tasks, and none of it equated to me learning what it took to be a man. I was conflicted on gender roles in an ignorant way because a man, in my mind, was a provider. All I could provide was a headache and an attitude.

To my mother, I'm sorry. I was wrong on every count. I took you for granted, too often not knowing how much of your life you dedicated to raising your children.

I put my mother through the wringer to the point she couldn't take it anymore. She called my father and told him of my misbehaving ways. I can imagine she hoped his male influence or using him as a fear tactic would instill some discipline in me. But it never did. I lacked respect for my father and even more for myself. I was talking back, questioning her decision-making, skipping school—just out of control in my teenage years. The only thing I did right was to maintain my grades. The only motivation my father provided stemmed from anger. He would call to tell me some of my male cousins of similar age to me were failing at life. One of them was a football star. He played quarterback at William M. Raines High School on the north side of Jacksonville. Then he started holding up people at gunpoint. Another had just earned himself a three-year prison sentence for peddling a controlled substance. The way my father phrased stories of my cousins was as if I were headed down a similar path. It infuriated me. I truly believe in those moments my sensitivity overshadowed the lessons my father intended on teaching me. Our relationship had become so fragile that everything he said bothered me. But I knew, regardless of what my cousins were going through, it had nothing to do with me. I couldn't fail my mother nor fail to receive my high school diploma.

High school graduation is a huge milestone for anyone. It's the bittersweet conclusion to your childhood years, full of cherished friends and memories. It's also the beginning of a new life chapter full of uncertainty and questions of what's next.

> *"I'm an adult now; do I get a job, join the military or go to college?*
> *Is my decision my own or to appease my family?*
> *What do I want?*
> *Who am I?*

My decision to attend college was easy; no other man in my family had ever before graduated with his degree. So I took it as a challenge, in which the odds were against me, and I figured going to college equated to success. As an African American male in 2009, I knew the dropout rate of blacks was 10.6% in comparison to my white counterparts at only 6.3%, according to the National Center of Education Statistics.[4] I was charged with defying the generational curse of educational deficiency and overwhelming statistics of failure. I would defy both.

On the morning of June 5, 2009, as I laid awake in bed and watched my 6am alarm go off, I just exhaled deeply, thinking today is mine; nothing can steal this joy. *"God, thank you for allowing me to be able to see another day and make it thus far in life. I ask that you continue to order my footsteps as I take on this next journey in life and protect me from danger seen and unseen in your son Jesus' name. Amen."* As I concluded my prayer, I took my time to get dressed because I wanted to savor every minute of this day. I turned to my computer to begin my routine musical therapy session and began with Common's *I Used to Love H.E.R.*

This song was the reason I fell in love with Hip-Hop music. The artist paints this sonic masterpiece of a woman going through many transformations while attempting to discover who she was by interacting with people of contrasting lifestyles. She struggled to bring all her experiences together, and the lack of self identity progressed into promiscuous adventures that carried her around from coast to coast. This woman's name was Hip-Hop. Common's story personified a whole genre of sound, giving listeners the history of how *she* expanded from its origins as new artists entered the game with their own influences.

This song was my Holy Grail track of Hip-Hop. It was a perfect representation of how I felt in that moment, just thinking where my life would take me over time as I stepped into a new world.

What influences will I fall to?
What kind of people will I meet?
Will I fit in?
How will I evolve and mature through my encounters in my new surroundings?

Common was not only giving listeners a deeper look into Hip-Hop, but also subconsciously encouraging his audience to be mindful of their maturation through life. You have a beginning and an ending, but what happens in between those two points is what creates your identity.

As I bobbed my head to the fresh tunes, I proceeded to get dressed in the outfit my mother had taken to the cleaners. Ripping through the plastic, I retrieved the freshly pressed black pinstriped Sean Jean slacks with matching five button vest and white-collared button up. I thought to myself *ooooh wee, I'm about to be too clean.*

I grabbed my mother's truck keys and headed to the Jacksonville Veterans Memorial Arena for my call time of 7:30am with the rest of the 2009 graduating class of Paxon School for Advanced Studies.

"Meezy, we made it, boy," Felix said as we began to line up in alphabetical order for our processional into the main arena. Felix was one of my few true friends in my graduating class. Most of my other friends were in older classes while others in younger. I really didn't gravitate to many kids in my class for a plethora of reasons. I felt I couldn't relate to them. I was overly critical of them and their choices. I judged more than I cared to learn about my classmates and the rationale behind decisions I felt were poor ones. But on this day, none of that mattered. I was happy for everyone who reached this pinnacle with me. That moment in time cemented our place in the history of Paxon alum. We were all decorated in our navy blue gowns, extending past our shins, stopping at the top of our ankles. The golden tassels illuminated the crown of our caps along with other gold accents across medals of student-led organizations and braided cords representing academic achievement. The arena lights shined as bright as movie lights on the set of a big Hollywood production. As we sat in our assigned seats, I looked across the crowd attempting the impossible task of locating my family amongst the sea of thousands of faces full of immeasurable elation. The stubbornness in me wouldn't accept not finding them until the time came for my row to get up and…walk across that stage.

Walking the stage represented a rite of passage. It was my departure from youth and the reckless decisions in childhood into adulthood, where I'd have to assume responsibility for all my choices moving forward. There wouldn't be any *redos, timeouts, uh ohs, wait a minutes,* or *let me ask my moms first.* Now, every decision made determined and defined my future. Truthfully, it scared me. I doubted the lessons I'd learned up to this point and didn't know how to put the knowledge I accumulated into action. The origin of my reluctance came from the unstable relationship with my father. I felt I had many untaught lessons about life that my mother couldn't teach me. Those unspoken conversations were the remaining puzzle pieces of my confidence to take on life. Trust within myself was something I did not have. I began overthinking every choice I made. But here goes nothing. *I'll figure it out…on my own.* If anything, I demonstrated just how inadequate my faith was in God. In his Word, 1 Corinthians 10:13 states:

> "No temptation has overtaken you that is not common to man. God is faithful, and he will not let you be tempted beyond your ability, but with the temptation he will also provide the way of escape, that you may be able to endure it."

This Scripture was my evidence that nothing to come my way would break, destroy, or kill me, but would instead empower me to exceed personal expectations. But at 18 and full of uncertainty, I didn't believe that Scripture held much value to my circumstances. Approaching my walk across that stage, my mind ran through all the pep talks from people whom I'd respected and whose opinions I valued—from my parents, uncle and cousins to my peers, some just a few years older than I.

Just apply yourself. Stay hungry and allow those gifts in you to touch this world. We need you.

The skies are the limit for you. All the potential you have and success is inevitable. Breathe, man; just breathe.

Nephew, I knew you could do it. The White House is next. I love you, man.

Cuz, we gone be all on UCF's campus on the chicks! Whew, just save some for me when I get down there.

There is nothing to worry about. You know what's next. You're going to college. Just think about how many graduating seniors absolutely don't know what tomorrow will be. They are the ones who should be worrying. You're going to college; smile, man!

Ish, your maturity will open a number of doors for you, but you have to trust the process and go have some fun. Live in the now. Yesterday is over; tomorrow will come.

And before I knew it, I was shaking the hand of my high school principal, posing for a picture. I failed to relish in that moment, so lost in thoughts of my future and knowing that experience would never happen again. It proved to be my first poor decision of adulthood. Exiting off stage, I proceeded to smile for more pictures, masking my internal battle while struggling to live in the now.

"Ladies and gentlemen, I present to you the 2009 graduating class of Paxon School for Advanced Studies," Mrs. Daniels, the school principal, announced. The crowd erupted in excitement. The time came to do the iconic cap toss to the heavens where our dreams were awaiting to introduce themselves to us. Gazing around as the caps ascended, time seemed to slow down. I caught myself forgetting about my worries and a smile instantly ensued. This is what it felt like to relax and celebrate the now. *I graduated high school. Like I really did it!*

Outside the arena, just as the heat of the day managed to roll in, I turned in my gown and found my family. "Boop, how does it feel to be a high school graduate?" my mom asked with the biggest smile across her face. That smile was the only diploma I cared to have. Seeing her overjoyed moved me into a great space mentally because I knew the frequent sacrifices she had made for me. This accomplishment may be viewed as an individual achievement with my name on it, but it was the team's win with not enough room on the diploma for all the names of those responsible for my earning it. My dad was there as well with a similar expression. But as I looked at his eyes, I could see that he'd been crying. I knew he was proud of me, and, to be honest, it was an unforgettable feeling. I was surrounded by so much love. Everyone was there to celebrate me—all three of my parents, including my stepfather, my sister, my grandmother, aunts, uncle, cousins and best friend, Jermaine. What else could I ask for? I was showered in congratulations, hugs, kisses, and thoughtful cards reminding me today…was mine!

We moved this celebration indoors to Mitchell's Fish Market, where the food was finger-licking good. My mother had the duty of booking the reservation to ensure everyone was accommodated. The party was large, more than 15 people, and reality hit me that this could turn bad at the drop of a dime. Having the privilege of uniting both sides of my family came with a deadly price. The mesh of personalities could clash at any minute. Each person having a different level of tactfulness, the slightest bit of sarcasm could be misinterpreted. I was nervous. In addition to my family and best friend, Jermaine, were my friends Karen, Cameron, and Andre. I had developed close friendships with all of them over the duration of my high school years. They always had my back; I appreciated them for being there.

Poopie, my stepbrother, was also able to make it. This meant a lot to me as well because he had also graduated from high school just a few days prior. Granted, we were brought together as total strangers, both protective of our respective parent and expected to accept one another's ways. To be completely transparent, Poopie was cool and approached the situation with openness. That type of maturity earned my respect, and we made it work ever since our parents' union in 2004. Maybe it worked because of our age or we were at a point in life where figuring out our *tomorrows* meant more than being overly critical of each other. Nonetheless, he took the time to step away from his own celebrations with his family, and his thoughtfulness spoke volumes to his character.

Sitting at dinner, I got that feeling again, the one in which I observe caps rise from the grasp of each graduate praying for answers, direction, and mental resolve over all. The feeling in which time manages to slow down, giving me the ability to understand just how instrumental this dinner was in bringing my families together. Everyone was on his and her best behavior, truly enjoying one another's company. This meant more to me than graduating high school. This may have been the first time I realized how much power I had in uniting people of varying opinions, experiences, and even different walks of life. Then the embarrassing stories started to roll in—and in alarming fashion. "Toni, do you remember that one time Ish ran into the wall because his head was so big? He never walked anywhere," my dad asked, failing to hold in his laughter. "The boy was running so damn fast and his head couldn't keep up with his feet. Then, before you knew it, BOOM. Listen, y'all. It took everything in me not to laugh. I said boy, 'slow the hell down, so you wouldn't fall.' Ish fell more than anyone I knew. It was crazy. But he never learned to stop running everywhere." As another anecdote started, I looked over to my friends who were fighting tears of laughter. And you know what, I didn't mind being the muse of humor tonight. I just wanted to use this night as an umbrella for a rainy day, giving me a reason to smile.

Making my way to my mother, I noticed she was uneasy, and I couldn't imagine why. "Mom, you okay? What's wrong?" I inquired.

"Nothing, baby. Just nothing," she replied, but I knew then she was hiding something. It was all over her face and in her tone, but I recognized asking again wasn't in my best interest. Retreating back to my seat, I pondered a million ideas as to what could be wrong. Looking down at my phone, I checked the time. I knew I had to stop by my girlfriend's festivities before it became too late. Part of me didn't want to leave without knowing what was causing my mother's unsettling mood, but I was in celebration mode. Nothing was going to stop this train. Selfishness in its glory and I felt as if I deserved a pass for my indulgence in self-desires just for tonight. Saying my goodbyes and passing out kisses like Mr. Hershey himself, I took more pictures and grabbed all of my presents. "Jermaine, you rolling with me?" The rhetorical question didn't require much because he was always at my side ready for all activities.

Jermaine was a year behind me in school, but it was as if we were separated at birth, and God brought us together at Paxon. He'd become my little brother, someone who accepted me for the flawed human being I was and actually thought I was worth hanging around. Everything about him brought out the best in everyone he encountered. With a huge personality and heart to match, he was definitely someone whose energy was needed in my life. His dedication to those he cared about could never be questioned because he'd go to the end of the world with you if he loved you. I feared I was incapable of returning that type of loyalty to him, but it was a quality I strove to learn from him. Our friendship taught me that one can learn from just about anyone, regardless of age. Jermaine was far beyond his years and, much like myself, he was blind to his true gifts. Our connection rested on the commonality of our life experiences. The ironic thing is everything I would go through, his life would also take him through the same tribulations. Noticing this undeniable pattern, I felt responsible for him—a responsibility to place my pride to the side and share with him my lowest moments. By articulating my pain, it gave me a sense of hope that he would be more equipped to maneuver through these troubles. Nothing could allow me to let him go through life without me pouring what I'd learned into him.

Exiting the restaurant and getting into my mother's red Ford Explorer, we were ready to get active. Our destination known, our spirits high, but what the night had for us was still an oblique mystery. Yet we had no complaints.

"Bro, how does it feel knowing you leaving the Ville soon," he asked.

"Honestly, it still hasn't hit me, but I'm glad. I'm over being here," I replied.

That was the last we spoke before our shared love for music took over the conversation. Getting on 9A, which turned into 295 East, heading towards Orange Park, we were getting Closer to Our Dreams with Ice "Billion" Berg. It was a remake of Gopale's hit, and he really transformed the song into his own, relating it to the rough streets of Miami and giving listeners insight on who Iceberg was. Displaying an ability to deliver a slower paced flow all while maintaining his grittiness through lyrics about how he "do it for the hustlers f*ck the otha side." In contrast, he kept the angelic voice of Goapele on the chorus and the conclusion of the song. It was a career-defining song for him as he took a risk for a sound he'd yet to attempt. Could I relate to the content? No, not at all, but I valued the uniqueness of his vocal inflections and the refreshing sound coming from Miami, which this was nothing like.

I was cruising down 295, doing about 70 the whole way to Brandy's house. And right as I was about to exit on Blanding, my phone rang. "Hello," I said, not bothering to look down to check who was calling.

"ISH…STOP Y'ALL, JUST STOP," it was my sister and she was frantic. I could hear the tears in her voice. She was overwhelmed with emotion, barely able get words out to talk to me.

"Monica, what's wrong? I need you to calm down," I replied in a state of shock. Before my mind started becoming the devil's jungle gym of activity, I needed an answer immediately, for my own emotional stability.

"It's mommy and Curtis…come home!" In the far distance, I could hear my mom yelling and just livid. "Son, I'm okay. Go enjoy your night," she said, taking the phone from my sister. From just that short response, I could tell it was a domestic issue between my mother and stepfather. I pulled over on the side of the highway and got out. I could feel the rage overtaking me. An internal heat raised my temperature. My stomach got tight. My face got stiffer than a dead body, and my heart pounded hard with anticipation.

If he touches her, he's dead.

And like that, graduation was irrelevant. It was a figment of the past. It did not have any value to me because it couldn't help me throw my life away. At the thought of my mother being hit or even pushed, I became committed to losing my freedom.

"Everything straight?" Jermaine asked. But I couldn't answer; words wouldn't formulate from my lips. Making the first of many mistakes that night, I jumped behind the wheel and mashed the gas pedal, continuing on to my girlfriend's house. Speeding down Blanding Boulevard, I exceeded 90 miles per hour. The speed limit was 45 mph. At that point, it was over for me. There was no such thing as thinking rationally; my emotions had taken full control. Swerving in and out of lanes, cutting people off—Jermaine just sat there quietly. Even to this day, I've yet to apologize for putting his life in danger and not asking how he felt. But in that moment, I didn't care. The only concern I had was for my mother and sister's safety. I had to protect them; it was my responsibility to do so. I couldn't let anything or anyone hurt them. For them, I'd kill.

Turning onto the street of Brandy's house, I saw a lady walking in the street. I just missed hitting her as I drove uncontrollably on the residential street. Ignoring her screams, I parked, jumped out of the car, and I could see recognizable faces, which I knew were Brandy's family members . Came to find out it was her aunt whom I'd nearly run over. "Ismael, what is wrong. Please talk to me. You almost…," Sonya, Brandy's mother, stopped when she saw the tears falling from my face. She knew something more powerful was in control. "You got to calm down and tell me what's going on?"

Ring, ring, ring. It was my phone going off, and it was my sister again. "Ish, they are fighting." And that was all I needed to push me off the cliff. Her words shattered my psyche. I knew soon enough I'd do something ungodly, unruly, something from which there was no turning back from. Truthfully, I was content with that. It was a part of my destiny. My heart palpitated, skipping a number of beats.

I trembled noticeably, and the tears kept rolling like a leaking faucet. "Ms. Sonya, I gotta go," I said as I reached for the truck keys.

"Ismael, I cannot let you go anywhere until you calm down. It's not safe for you to drive like this. Let's pray." As she talked, I blocked out everything she was saying. In that moment, I didn't want to pray or hear *it's going to be okay*. I just wanted to go home. My mind was creating elaborate scenarios about what could be going on in my absence and what would transpire when I got there.

> *Hope he ready to meet the devil because I'm sending him to hell on a one way.*
> *I don't care if I gotta go with him my damn self.*
> *I can't wait to stand over his body and watch his blood run.*
> *Yeah, I'm claiming one tonight, earning my stripes.*

Out the side of my eye, Brandy stood there speechless. Never before seeing me like this must have terrified and shocked her. This was happening on what should have been the happiest moment of her life. And to think I was beyond pissed with her, I felt she didn't show enough concern. I was too drunk on myself to acknowledge her feelings. "Well, can Jermaine drive?" I snapped in response to me leaving. I just had to get home before it was too late.

> *What if mom is hurt? Then it's going to be Ms. Sonya's fault.*
> *How she gone explain to me that things are going to be okay and God is protecting my mom and sister if they are in the hospital?*

Attempting to outsmart Ms. Sonya, I had to give off the impression that I was calming down and regaining logical thinking. *Ring, ring, ring*, again. My hands shook, unsteadily trying to retrieve my phone from my pocket. This time, it was my mother...

"Hey…Boop…," she greeted breathing heavily. "I just wanted to…let you know…we are fine. You know your mom can take care of herself. Curtis is gone. Don't worry. God got us. Don't come home. Enjoy your night. We are fine." Her words eased my evil thinking, slightly. But it didn't register to me why she didn't want me to come home.

Did she not realize I was their protector, their wolf in sheep's clothing, ready to sacrifice myself for them?

"Mom, I am coming home as soon as I can drive," I responded. "Ismael, you do what I said. Do you hear me? Enjoy yourself tonight. You worked too hard for this. Don't be stupid, son," she countered.

"Yes, ma'am. I love you. I'll let you know when I'm on the way."

"Son, I love you too." Click.

As the level of rage descended, I walked into the house under the agreement that after I watched a movie with Brandy and her family, I could leave. This was an even compromise in my mind. It allotted me the time to gather myself, spend time with someone I cared deeply about, and I loved movies. Stepping into the bathroom, I wiped my face, looked in the mirror, and quickly turned away before I was able to really focus the image reflected back. I didn't want to capture what I saw. In the moment, I doubted I could handle what was projected back to me. Drying my hands, I exited, and let thoughts linger in my head.

Am I really capable of acting on everything I feel?
Would I be more of a man if I did?
Less if I didn't?

"Ismael, you feeling better? Thought I seen a smile peak out," Ms. Sonya asked. And to be honest, I did feel better. She and I would talk a few more minutes until I realized I didn't have my glasses on. I managed to leave them in the truck and really couldn't see much. "Ms. Sonya, imma step out real quick and get my glasses. You know I'm blind."

"Don't play with me and try to leave," she replied. "No, ma'am, not at all. Plus I couldn't leave Jermaine," I stated half joking. As I walked outside, I took a deep breath of fresh air. Before she'd said it, I hadn't even thought about going back home. But the inception of the idea did sound appealing. *I could go make sure my family is safe for my own sanity. Jermaine would understand.* Stepping off the driveway and past the "Congratulations Graduate" sign, I crossed the street. I thought about just how much of a forgotten moment graduation now was. As I got closer to the truck, I saw glass scattered across the pavement. I stood still for a minute, trying to process what exactly was going on. I wasn't even sure if it was safe to continue to approach the truck to investigate. Then I slowly walked closer, scanning every which way for signs of who or what could have done this.

Really? You gotta be kidding me!

I'd been robbed. Opening the door, more glass fell to the ground. Whoever had done it took the brasher route instead of just picking the lock. The driver's side window was smashed in. Trying to analyze the level of the stolen score, I searched for what all else was missing. And not surprisingly, they had taken everything—the unopened graduation cards, GPS, CDs, all gone. At that point, the rage I felt an hour ago came back in full force. It was in that very second that I realized there was no further question as to what I was capable of doing. I now knew—I could do anything my mind could conceive. I hopped out of the truck and furiously slammed the door. Even more glass poured out, a couple of pieces bouncing off the pavement, hitting me in the face, barely missing my eyes. I stared at that shattered glass, admiring the likeness we shared. The similarities were unparalleled.

How can this s**t get any worse?
Somebody must pay for this.
Yeah…someone will.

I guess the jig was up. Ms. Sonya thought I tried to pull a fast one on her. She came outside along with Jermaine, Brandy and a few other family members. As they got closer, I knew they could see the evil looming over me. I was just a vessel for multiple demons, ready to confiscate my life and soul. The demonic voices got louder in my head, transforming from low whispers of what I could just make out the words to a crescendo of thunderous roars reaching the peak of it's break, deafening me from what anyone around me was saying. Standing there empty inside, I absorbed their stares while still looking at that glass, mindlessly.

You know what to do.
This sh*t ain't over.

"They stole my shoes," Jermaine said with apparent disappointment. His voice was the only one able to pierce through the sound barrier of the demonic conversations being held within the confines of my head.

Not only did they rob you, they got your little brother.
The one you claimed you would protect and look after.

You weak f*ck! You can't protect anybody.
First you let a man do God knows what to your mom while your
sister watched and now this.
You ain't no man until you do something.
Somebody got to die. Yeah, that's it; somebody must die.

"Call the police," someone suggested. We would soon learn we weren't the only victims of a vehicular break-in. One of Brandy's aunts was also the recipient of criminal recklessness. "We got to file reports for insurance. Lord, have mercy. The devil is busy. It's going to be okay, though," one other victim preached. I didn't see the purpose in calling the cops. They weren't going to find the guys who did this or retrieve the stolen items. And because of the stigma carried by being black, the cops' arrival time would be slower. A sense of urgency would not exist. For that matter, I figured I'd be questioned as the prime suspect. They would only annoy me further and support my reasoning for taking matters into my own hands. I shook myself and then thought to call my cousin. He'd be down to get active in these streets and find whoever did this.

My cousin, whom I won't identify here, was someone who was a direct product of his environment—growing up on the north side of Jacksonville, in the heart of a most crime-invested neighborhood. It was actually a miracle he had lived to the age of 20, given all the violent activities he'd been involved in and survived. He lived an unruly, broken life full of rotating male figures who were in and out of the penitentiary system or had fallen victim to the block's cold kiss of death. It was that passion of a life for which the outcome was a box—whether it came with bars or buried under six feet of dirt, the box connected them. My cousin was someone I knew I couldn't hang around much because we walked two different paths and were from two different worlds. But after that night, I was feeling ready to dabble in his.

Ring, ring, ring…no answer. I could come back to my senses and understand I was attempting to be something I wasn't built for. But by this time, I couldn't decipher what was me or of my character. The struggle of self-definement versus self-preservation or the debate of *nature* versus *nurture* was at hand. The core of self and my innate qualities intertwined and were to walk a straight path—never even questioning, making poor decisions, living a life I didn't have to. The street life, in my opinion, was lived by those who weren't granted the choice or liberties to visually observe other ways of life. Growing up, I was blessed enough to optically consume a variety of options in living—high school graduates, college dropouts, drug peddlers and users, state property statesmen, and salaried 9 to 5'ers.

By seeing different paths, I was able to acquire information that allowed me to see where each would lead me. Being able to take from each gave me breadth of knowledge without having to make the same decisions or choices others had made. I learned to build my foundation of opportunity brick by brick, each piece consisting of what I'd studied and learned from others. My observations and research, in addition to my mother's determination to steer me away from certain troubles, kept me on a positive path. Deep down inside, I couldn't stomach prison. The stories my uncle would recollect were reinforcement of how hard it was behind those iron bars. Even stories from television shows and movies helped me to understand prison life. Truth be told, I wasn't built for such a life, and going to prison was one of my greatest fears. But after being subjected to domestic violence and a loss of joy, I was ready for whatever consequences followed my actions—even prison.

Ring, ring, ring…my cousin picked up on my second attempt. "Cuz, I got robbed," I pleaded. I could tell from the background noise he was at some party because I could hear an overwhelming amount of music, which interfered with our conversation.

"Cuz, I can't hear you. Say it again," he yelled back into his phone.

"I said, some niggas got me—came up on a lick off my graduation stuff, over on Blanding. I need your help, man. And you know I don't call you unless it's serious." This time he could hear me loud and clear. His reply was stern and empty in feeling. I knew what I'd done and felt no sorrow. "I'm at this party right now, cuz. But just chill out. Imma put my ear to the block and see what I can find out. I got you. But, man, you chill. Leave this alone. This ain't you!" My patience was completely gone with people telling me *who I was.* Even I didn't know in this moment. All I could think about was how weak I must have looked to everyone.

> *No one thinks I can handle my own, huh?*
> *Just the schoolboy who gets punked.*
> *Naw, they will see what I'm made of when faced with the madness.*
> *I'll go out fighting in a blaze before I fall victim to another man.*
> *I got me and forget who opposes.*

All I could do was listen to my cousin. He knew more about these types of situations than I did. Getting high on emotions would get me hurt or even worse…killed. So I took the backseat here to someone more experienced and driven by logic over emotional plight. The essence of self-definement—nurture—would champion my actions in a situation in which self-preservation—nature—was being challenged.

Hanging up the phone in disappointment, I just hopped into the truck, waiting for the cops to arrive. Calmness started to overcome everyone through conversation and a few laughs, which took everyone's mind off the horrid. Even I cracked a few smiles. I looked at Brandy with an eagle eye, just hoping for her to console me; however, it never came. She didn't realize how much power she had, and how she could be the bright spot in all of the darkness circling in on me.

After 35 minutes, the world's most unreliable police officers of Jacksonville's Sheriff Office arrived to the scene of the crime. "Okay, what is the problem here?" one of them asked.

"Sir, it's pretty clear what the problem is here. Don't you see all this glass on the ground?" I replied sternly, not giving an ounce of cooperation to them. It was evident to me they didn't want to be here, dealing with this problem, no more than I did through our exchanges full of sarcasm and the absence of respect for one another.

"Officer, it took y'all over half an hour to get here, and you want me to be calm and relax?" I continued.

"Son, I'm going to need you to check your tone. We are here to help you. We're going to investigate the situation and fill out a report," he insisted. Just because he said *we're going to investigate the situation* did not mean it created a sense of ease. It was comedic to me. I knew they couldn't really do anything as was evident by the fact they conducted a walk-through investigation and made obvious observations like, "This is where they entered with brute force."

No duh, dumbass.
The glass everywhere is clearly an indicator of forced entry.
Where did you get your badge?
A Cracker Jack box.

After another 10 minutes of "investigating," Officers Dumb and Dumber expertly concluded we were victims of neighborhood sweepers—a description of criminals who happen to have ample time on their hands to case or survey an area for an extended period of time before striking, knowing precisely when no one will be around. They were your everyday opportunists.

"Must've spotted the graduation signs outside of your house, ma'am, and saw a gold mine. A quick smash and grab, in and out in less than 3-5 minutes flat. We see this all the time, especially around the holidays," Officer Dumber informed us. "If you could just sign here, I'll give you both copies of the report for your insurance so damage claims can be filed. Enjoy your evening and be safe folks," he continued, walking away to my relief. The sooner they left, the best chance I had at not making more unwarranted comments that could possibly lead me to become a victim of police brutality or a ride in their back seat headed directly to county jail.

"Well, everyone, I'm going home. I got to figure out a way to explain this to my mother after all the crap she's dealt with tonight," I said with a sarcastic smirk. Sweeping all of the remaining glass out of the driver seat, I was given a towel to sit on by Ms. Sonya as an extra safety precaution. I strapped on my seat belt, cranked up the engine, and sped off into the night. By this time, it was well after midnight. The night air had cooled and the sky was dark with no stars in sight. It was reflective of what I felt on the inside—nothing. Not even 5 minutes after speeding off, Jermaine was sleep. It had been a long emotional night. I also wanted to do the same. With a broken truck window, I felt every degree of the cool night air chilling more and more as I pressed the gas pedal harder.

> But I'm going higher
> Closer to my dreams
> I'm going higher and higher
> I can almost reach

Goapele's lyrics resounded in my mind: *but I'm going higher,* the allure of accomplishing a goal I set for myself. *Closer to my dreams,* a dream not yet vivid enough for optic admiration, but a step towards the dream, nonetheless, was achieved. *I'm going higher and higher,* I was college bound. How could I forget the significance of that?

The lyrics also reminded me of how close I was to my dream just to see it go up in flames. The song spoke to me in that moment, giving me a sense of pride in my recent accomplishment, yet reinforcing that my dreams were still in reach no matter the grief I was experiencing.

*****

It was Sunday morning when I thought the nightmare was over. My mom as usual would come wake up my sister and me for church. On this particular Sunday morning, I laid in bed restless. Lost in my thoughts, replaying my undesirable yet eventful weekend. Shaming myself with blame that I allowed another man to cause harm to my mother and letting some busters rob me.

> *You so damn weak and everyone knows it.*
> *That's why you getting played.*
> *You want to call yourself a man, but can't protect your damn self.*

My thoughts wouldn't allow me to look at these situations from a practical standpoint, accepting the truth that I had done no wrong. These incidents could have happened to anyone, but my pride had been wounded. I thirsted for blood. I could taste the warm saltiness all over my taste buds, inciting joy across my appetite for a moment of violence. I felt the need to redeem myself for displaying lesser characteristics of a *two-fisted thoroughbred man*.

I imagined this is how Mitch from the movie *Paid In Full* felt sitting in the car with his best friend and co-conspirator, known as A, pouring out his heart from the kidnapping of his little brother. You see, the only thing Money Makin Mitch loved more than money itself was little Sonny. He was the one thing on this Earth that had done him no wrong and for whom he assumed responsibility. Sonny motivated Mitch to grind, work harder, and stay in the drug dealing game to create a better life for his little man. Sonny proved to be Mitch's one weakness because in one scene of the movie viewers get to visualize the distress he was experiencing, knowing there was nothing he could do.

As the tears poured down his face, Mitch embodied the same feeling and mental angst I had. The anticipation of revenge was the only thing that could fulfill my desire. I wanted to assure myself that I was capable of offering protection to my family and myself. I didn't want things to come to the point where I'd be without my mother or sister in the same light as Mitch without Sonny. Knowing I wasn't there to prevent harm to them or fight their battles made me feel dead on the inside, and I was willing to be *on some murder sh*t,* too.

I was always warned to be careful about what I wish or pray for because it'll come to pass when you least expect it. And my wish came in the form of loud knocks at the door. "It's okay, Boop, lie down, don't answer," my mom reassured me as she walked over to my bedroom window to check outside for any sign of who was at the door. As she moved away from the window, she didn't say anything and gave me no idea of who it was, and she gingerly made her way towards the front door, yelling, "Who is it?" as the knocks continued, louder and more frequently. Before she could ask again, I heard a loud BOOM as the front door vehemently broke through its resting place. My mother screamed. The sun shined through the foyer, but there was nothing bright about this moment, in which only the darkness of my demons would flourish here. The blood rushed to my heart as the adrenaline kicked in, and I rushed to her defense, dressed in pajama pants, socks and a t-shirt. I had no time to think. There was only time to attack whoever it was.

Putting me at a disadvantage, I shut off my brain and negated any thoughts of whether this person had a gun, knife or anything other than his fist. It didn't matter to me. This was that moment of violence I craved deep down in the pit of my famished stomach.

Storming to the door with both hands up, I was determined to abolish whatever ignorant soul was stupid enough to kick in my front door. They had a death wish, and on this particular Sunday, I was a genie granting all wishes. As I got to the door, Curtis, my stepfather, was the one who decided to meet me in the arena where one of us had to fall. Exactly what I wanted. I couldn't have been more grateful but, of course, nothing favorable can come of destructive aspirations. Behind him were four of the finest from the Sherriff's Office.

So what, f*ckem!

Personally, I didn't care if he had a swat team with him. This was my moment. Yes, my moment of violence. I refused to give up this moment. No one could steal this away from me. It was mine! I threw the first punch, forcing Curtis to stumble backwards. I was the underdog in this fight as he was about 6'2" and 240-plus pounds. I knew one blow from him would finish me, and I couldn't allow him to connect any blows. I threw a flurry of punches, landing them all. Headshots, body shots—anywhere I could connect.

"STAND DOWN NOW," one of the officers commanded as another tried to tackle me to the ground. Pushing the officer off, I continued throwing punches. In the far background, I could hear my sister screaming from the front door as she was subjected to seeing two people she loved attack each other. One with intentions of hurting the other severely while the other wanted it all to end immediately.

What is Monica going to think of me?
How would my actions affect her image of me?
Will she fear me?
Will she think I'll harm her?

"STOP now or you will be taken down with force," the officer continued after seeing there was no stopping me with vocal instructions. My disdain for law enforcement was already on the rise because of the lack of urgency displayed when I got robbed of all my graduation gifts, my mother's electronic possessions, and Jermaine's things. There was no chance I was listening to any officer telling me anything.

"I'm an officer. I'm an officer," my mom shouted back.

"Ma'am, back away," the female officer instructed my mother as she attempted to calm down the officers before any overly aggressive actions were taken against me. My belligerent ways could have earned me a few rounds pumped into my body. On that day, Ismael could have been no more. Ismael could of turned into #JusticeForIsmael or #IsmaelBrown because police brutality for people of color is a real issue in America.

Before I knew it, two officers double-teamed me, slamming me onto the grass on my front yard. "I said calm down, son," one officer yelled at me with one knee on my back and a forearm pressed firmly against my neck. Managing to slip from under his grasp, I threw one last punch at my stepfather, causing him to fall. Then before I knew it, I was again being slammed by the same two officers—this time on concrete. My adrenaline wouldn't allow me to feel the brute force exerted on me, but I could feel the warm blood begin to flow down my left arm. Then all of a sudden my body felt an indescribable pain shoot through it.

"Put your damn hands down," the officer shouted in my ear with the same vantage point as before as he hit me again with what I found out later was a Taser. Immediately, I lost all motor skills.

"I'M DONE...stop, please stop...just stop," I desperately yelled out not wanting to be hit again, and sure thing he did it anyway.

"You, shut up. I'll stop when you stop," he replied. After another hit with the volt of instantaneous pain, I laid on top of the concrete of my driveway in disbelief. That concrete where my head came to rest collected my tears, saliva, and blood in a pool of moisture with fragments from the broken wood of our front door. Staring through pleading eyes, I caught a blurry vision of my family, completely broken and destroyed as they watched the police have their way with me. My sister was crying like a confused and disoriented newborn while my mother appeared defeated. She was beyond disappointed in her colleagues' handling of the situation and worried about her son. No mother wanted to ever see her son in a physical altercation, let alone with her husband and soon to be in the back of a cop car headed to jail. It was every mother's worst nightmare.

The two officers, exhausted and out of breath from their all-out exertion, picked me up and forcefully walked me over to the back of one of their cars. The cuffs gripped my wrists with no room for wiggling or any subtle movements. The backseat wreaked of old musk and an overwhelming combination of vomit and urine. The seats were not built for comfort for obvious reasons and were firmer than the concrete I had just come to rest on. The partition was composed of black crossbars and what I believed to be shatterproof glass. I could see on the other side the standard issued shotgun with eight shell casings to its side, ready for reloading. The dash consisted of a workstation with a laptop stand, night light, radio and clipboard and multiple pens. After analyzing the composition of the interior of the vehicle, I dropped my head. I couldn't stomach gazing out the window, longing for something no longer mine…freedom. I refused to take in any more cinematic views of my mother's aching heart uncontrollably purging itself. Nor could I consume the image of my sister making eye contact and looking right into my empty soul. And I, without question, denied Curtis the satisfaction of claiming victory in the war in which I'd fallen in defeat, not even glorifying the sweet taste of winning the battle.

I just sat there staring back into a life with no outcome. It was bleak, frigid and resulting in nothingness. College would be no more; getting a job would be near impossible. I was soon to become the statistic I'd vowed never to be. According to the Report of The Sentencing Project to the United Nations Human Rights Committee Regarding Racial Disparities in the United States Criminal Justice System of 2013, it states:

> African-American males are six times more likely to be incarcerated than white males and 2.5 times more likely than Hispanic males. If current trends continue, one of every three black American males born today can expect to go to prison in his lifetime, as can one of every six Latino males—compared to one of every seventeen white males.[5]

The Sentencing Project is an organization founded in 1986. It works toward a fair yet effective U.S. criminal justice system by promoting reforms in sentencing policy, addressing racial disparities and practices, and advocating for alternatives to incarceration. In my situation, I guess I fulfilled that statistic since I was headed to the county jail.

> *Guess this the beginning of the end, huh?*
> *My whole life I avoided trouble in hopes to be something different.*
> *A role model for the kids, giving them hope.*
> *One of the ones who broke the stereotype and made it out of this madness.*
> *I was black, though. This was my destiny.*
> *How could I deviate from what I was born to do?*

My thoughts swirled until the cop got in and we drove off, then the tears returned. I was scared beyond measure; I had no other way to describe it. This was the only time I gave myself a pass on demonstrating a sign of weakness. But I had no regrets nor did I want to handle the situation any differently. For Toni and Monica, I'd lay down my life for them with my head held high to the heavens. For them, my life would be an honorable sacrifice I didn't mind making. I was their martyr.

I recalled the stories uncle Magic had told me about his time in prison. I wasn't built to do one second on the inside. Literally, I wanted to crawl into a fetal position and cry, but that wasn't an option for this new reality. As we exited the back of my neighborhood, heading down Hartsfield road, I lifted my head, taking mental photos of each and everything we passed on by—the trees, power lines, street lights not yet on, and the birds that flew in unison with one another. Then there were the kids riding bikes under the supervision of their parents, all staring at me like an animal at the zoo. I imagined the parents using me as a conversational piece on why they should behave, get good grades, and stay in school. Otherwise, they'd end up like me, a jailbird. I cried even more, thinking about how I was once that kid whose parents instilled those very principles. My tears fell in silence; there was no sobbing in an attempt to maintain some essence of toughness. They were the size of raindrops, soaking up my grass-stained pajama pants, covered in wood splinters and dirt.

Before we reached the intersection of Hartsfield and Merrill, we unexpectedly turned into the shopping plaza where the locals could find Bono's Bar-B-Que, Food Lion grocery store that's now a Wal-Mart, and other retail shops selling their products and services.

What's going on?
Why did we stop?
What's going to happen to me?

The officer backed into a distant parking space at the back of the Krystal's Burger parking lot. He just sat there, with a disgusted look on his face. I sat there quietly trying to gain insight as to what was going on. Not even five minutes had passed by when another officer, who was also at my house, pulled up next to us. Letting down his window, he said, "So how are we going to write this one up? This whole situation went bad quickly. We got to make sure we're all on the same page here."

"I know for damn sure we can't report anything about giving permission to kick in the door. That motherf*cker did that on his own, and that can't fall back on us. Let's just leave it out of the report," the officer chauffeuring me around replied.

I sat back, perplexed they would have this conversation with me sitting in the backseat listening to everything. But then again who would believe me? I was the one in cuffs and, oh yeah, I'm a black male younger than 25. I was what America feared. The officer was always right. Their conversation made me sick to my stomach to see how an injustice could be carried out and go unnoticed after so many years of oppression. We still were victims. "Still held back I done paid with my skin," as said by Pusha T on the Intro of *Darkest Before Dawn: The Prelude.* As a black male, he details the ceilings placed over him because of the color of his skin.

Victims sold false realities of equality, promised freedom from plantations in exchange for the captivity of prison wards across the nation that never loved us, just used us. These white officers felt no remorse in their evil hearts. They cared more about protecting their jobs than my life, which was now blemished with a criminal record—the equivalent of having leprosy in bible times, an outcast. It was my first real experience with just how much things had not changed since the times of the Civil Rights movement of the 1960s. As an African American male, life as a whole was an injustice, better did not exist.

"Let's get his ass downtown, and get him booked," the officer driving me said. The ride to the county jail gave me time to get my emotions in check and prepare myself for whatever awaited me on the inside. Whether it was more police excessive force or proving myself in a fight with fellow inmates, I had to acclimate rapidly. Arriving at the intake back door, the officer didn't hesitate to remind me how powerless I was.

"Welcome to my house, boy. Let's see you try that tough shi*t in here. There are plenty of tougher dudes in here waiting on someone like you, ready to break you in."

My heartbeat sped up drastically. I couldn't control it. He opened up the heavy steel door where his colleagues awaited my arrival with smirks on their faces. The first to insult me was an older African American officer with a black pepper buzz cut with speckles of grey hair. "Ahh, you look familiar. I know you done been in here before. Still out here being a dumbass getting in trouble."

"I ain't never been in jail before," I blurted out in response to his uneducated assertion. I loathed that he was degrading a young brother like myself who actually could use some positivity, but he was no better than the white officers who delivered me to this hellhole.

"Boy, you better take that volume down and lose the bass before I help you get rid of it," he replied, swiftly getting in my face and putting his hands on me with intentions of exerting force to control me.

"You take these cuffs off, I'll give you the same thing they got," I popped off without thinking about where I was or what they could do to me. At that moment, I began to buy into the new lifestyle I was destined for, the one with no outcome. The cloudy, somber life filled with silence in a world overrun by those who whispered in the dark, not wanting to be seen nor heard.

I just couldn't let another man disrespect me anymore, so I made it a point to let it be known. Before he could threaten me further, the officer behind the control panel interjected. "He's not lying. He's never been in trouble. His name doesn't come up in our system."

Hemmed up still by the male black officer, he got closer and whispered in my ear, "You lucky these cameras are on, or I'd beat you unconscious until your own mother couldn't recognize you. You ungrateful little f*ck." I was enraged and wanted nothing more than to prove who was the superior warrior in hand-to-hand combat.

As I continued through the intake process, stripping me of everything from my clothes to my identity as Ismael Brown, I became inmate number 561094. The reality sunk in deeper by the minute. As an 18-year-old, by society's standards, no one here cared if I still felt and acted like a boy. I was just another nigga, to be trapped in the system, running on the hamster wheel of injustice and forever identified as a menace. Then out the corner of my eye there appeared my grandmother, a former correctional officer of 20-plus years—and Dad. My heart fluttered. It was such a relief to see anyone who knew I wasn't a troubled, lost soul, but a young man caught in a situation of defending his family. Both of them were visibly upset, struggling to remain under control and hold their emotions in for the sake of the circumstances. It made no sense to act rowdy. I was in the hands of the law. So, I had to undergo the procedural steps of the law.

"Can we get my grandson pushed to today's court docket?" My grandmother asked the commanding officer on duty. "Sorry, Brown. But it's full, and we can't get him a court date until tomorrow morning," the officer replied.

> *What does she mean I can't get a court date until the morning?*
> *I can't stay the night in here.*
> *I don't know if I can make it.*
> *Why is this happening to me?*

My father embraced me. He knew how defeated I was mentally, hearing that news, and just embraced me. It was beyond comforting.

He and I didn't share many moments like this, thus it made all the difference. "Son, it's gone be alright; trust me. You hear what I say?"

No, dad. It's not going to be alright. I didn't do anything. Why me? Why is this happening to me? I thought to myself. I looked up to his eyes where confined tears refused to formulate, revealing compassion for his only son. "Yes, sir," I replied, knowing good and well I did not believe him at all.

"Give him an orange jumpsuit and put him in an isolated cell so nobody won't mess with him," my grandmother requested. The blessing in all of this was she had spent her whole career in the same facility where I was going to be housed in for the night. She was well respected and revered by her colleagues, so they granted her request. She was able to ensure I wouldn't go to general population and knew all the officers who would be on guard that particular night, officers who could also keep an eye on me.

"Put this on, boo. Orange jumpsuits are for violent offenders, so it'll keep people away from you, knowing you may hurt them," my grandmother told me. I proceeded to change into my new identity as violent offender 561094, waiting to incite fear because it was all I knew to survive. Fear is what I was full of and the only thing I could return to the environment around me. Fear is probably what filled a great percentage of the fellow inmates in this place. The fear of hunger, fear of economic strife, fear of ridicule, and fear of pursuing a path other than what their environment produced. "You gone have to stay the night, baby. You will be alright. Just be tough, baby," my grandma said with sternness in her voice.

> *There it goes again—that phrase, "You will be alright."*
> *Why does everyone not in these shackles keep saying that?*
> *How do they know it'll be alright? Huh?*
> *Are their hands swollen twice the normal size, are they still*

bleeding from the foreman or forced to fabricate an animalistic mantra to protect themselves?

No, they weren't. They couldn't get me out of here, so I was able to be home.

My ungratefulness was overflowing because no one could get me out of jail. I felt wronged and above having to spend any time in jail. I was embarrassed, ashamed, and even more so—humiliated. As I was escorted away from my grandmother and father, I looked at them with barren hopeless eyes, knowing this was something I had to deal with alone—just that, alone. Alone to face the night of the unknown. Taking one last glance at them as I was approaching a corner, I could see my dad's mouth, "Hold your head. It's gone be alright."

While walking down those long and wide white hallways outlined with out-of-bounds lines designed to restrict the movement of inmates, I kept my head down. I didn't want to make any direct contact with anyone. Didn't want anyone to notice my discomfort, let alone the fear flooding out from my pores. I didn't want to appear weak. "Just be tough, baby," the advice my grandmother gave me echoed in my mind. But I didn't exactly know what she meant to be tough. I was too numb to feel anything, let alone be tough. "Open door four," the officer said as she nudged me into my hole. "Spread your legs," she continued her instructions as she took the shackles off my ankles and waist. Removing those metal constrictors made me feel less of an animal and gave me some relief. "Close door four," she shouted back to the officer at the helm of the control panel. Locked behind the thick steel vault-like door, I was still handcuffed as she gave me one last instruction, "Stick your hands through the food tray." That was the last I would see of her for the remainder of my stay. I remained frozen, staring out from the 6" x 6" glass window, taking it all in, realizing this wasn't a dream. And it hit me deep down in my gut. The glass window allowed me to see only the control room where the officers maintained communication, surveillance, and commanded the switchboard to open and close cell doors. The floors were white as snow, and the surrounding hallways were crowded with conversation, but no visible bodies accompanied the voices.

> "I'm innocent."
> "It wasn't even my gun."
> "I need to call my lawyer."
> "OFFICER, I NEED A MEDIC."
> "Wait till lunch nigga, don't worry."
> "I'm from 5020, ain't no b*tch in…"

My newfound toughness was devoured by emotions, causing instant weakness in my knees, resulting in me collapsing. Dizziness ensued followed by nausea. I wanted to ignore everything I heard, but this was happening. There was no ignoring anything. I scanned my cell for the nearest hole to lose the contents of my stomach. Then I realized it wasn't a cell at all, contrary to my thoughts of jail. It was more of an isolation box. The box was 13 feet long by seven feet wide, with a small bed, sink, and a toilet not even a foot away from the bed and sink. I surged to the toilet, praying I didn't miss and vomit anywhere else. I felt claustrophobic and desperately in need of air and water. But this wasn't home, where I could just go outside to breathe the cool, fresh air of the Sunday morning nor could I walk over to my refrigerator and grab a refreshing drink of cold water. None of that was a reality for me anymore, only a reminder of my horrible situation.

After puking stomach acids, since I had no food in my belly at all, I swallowed long and hard to relieve the acidic burning taste from my esophagus. I took the time to regain my equilibrium before standing back up. I wiped my mouth of any residual saliva and my eyes of the lingering tears of fear. *Just be tough, baby,* my grandma's voice replayed, and I said to myself, "No more tears."

Man up!
Quit being so soft; you actin like a female right now.
So what you locked up?
Stick your chest out, hold your head up, and do this lil time.
This easy!

I sat on the bed just looking around, hoping to find any reason to relax and put my mind at ease. I felt I was combatting the time in jail and my mind in a 2-on-1 match-up. Outnumbered and unprepared, I was going to make this situation worse than what it was.

Before I could further drag myself into the depths of my mind, I heard a knock, and a face appeared to peep in looking at me. I stood up and stared back, realizing it was a fellow inmate wearing a trustee's grey jumpsuit. No emotion rested on my face. I clinched my fist, staring back and showing I was no punk. My heart raced, but I refused to let my guard down. I didn't want any trouble, but if it was brought my way, I had to defend myself. We said nothing to each other, just a staring contest until a guard ordered the inmate to move on. I locked in on the inmate until he was out of sight from my 6" x 6" window.

It's either him or me.
That's the mindset you gotta have up in here.
Survival of the fittest; you gone get down or lay down!

I was prepared to stand ten toes down, ready to take my respect because I didn't know to what else to do.

I seemed to have adapted quickly to the way of life of an inmate, eager to prove my manhood. Deep down, this was in no form or fashion a reflection of my character or who I was raised to be. It was an effect of being behind those walls, denying your freedom, being weighed down by chains, encompassed by so much displaced testosterone. Your mentality shifts once you're inside the devil's house. Your awareness is at an all time high. All your thoughts prompted towards evil, and your hope dwindles by the heartbeat.

Again another knock at the steel door, but this time it was a male officer, "You got a visitor. Place your hands through the tray." This was unexpected to be honest, but I needed something to free me of the whispers all throughout the devil's house. As I emerged from my box, back in handcuffs, I was ready to hold my head up and eyeball anybody who walked by. By now, I had fully brought into my thoughts that I knew what I was doing. I stopped being soft and became stupid thinking. The officer walked me into the visiting room and sat me down in a chair. I had my own phone receiver to pick up and speak to the person behind the protective glass. To the right of me was another inmate, much larger than I was and also in an orange jumpsuit. Then the fear crept back in as we connected eyes. I quickly turned away, giving away the first sign of weakness to him. I refocused my attention towards the phone receiver, picking it up as my dad walked in and did the same. As soon as I heard his voice, the tears mounted in my eyes. The both of us knew I wasn't made for this life nor good at pretending to be.

He placed his hands around his mouth and the phone's receiver and said, "Son, don't you cry. If he sees it, he gone try you." I knew exactly who "he" was, that larger human being not even two chairs away from me who was at least 6'2" and 240-plus pounds, dressed in the orange jumpsuit. "I know you scared, but now ain't the time to show it. You gotta be strong until we can figure this out. I talked to your mom. She's okay, so stop worrying. She's actually on her way up here," my dad continued.

"Yes, sir," I replied.

"When you talk, put your hand over the receiver, so they can't see what you're saying. You gone be in here at least until tomorrow. Your granny got you on the first court docket in the morning. Don't cry, boy!"

My tear ducts flooded at the very moment I was reminded I had to stay the night. All I could say again was, "Yes, sir." The more I heard his voice, the more I wanted to just hug him and cry on his shoulder. We didn't have the best relationship, but at the moment none of our differences mattered because he was there for me. We would chat for another four minutes about any and everything else just to alleviate the stress of my current state. His words eased my mind a bit, but truthfully I was more concerned with not letting any tears fall and having to deal with this hungry bear next to me. I could feel his eyes watching me, waiting for any indication that I was weak.

"Stand tall, hold your head, and it'll be over soon," my dad said as we hung up the receivers, and I was off, back to my isolation box. I didn't look in the direction of the bear. Figured it was the same as the walker of the woods, waiting to lock his sights on prey. I dragged along in my shackles. Arriving back at my hole, I then went through the same process of sticking my hands through the food tray to be released of handcuffs. I sat on my bed and stared at the wall. Hunger pains began to creep into the bottom half of my stomach, and I tried to block out thoughts of food. I was in jail; food should have been the last thing on my mind.

I stood up to re-examine my quarters. There wasn't much I missed at all initially. Everything was in such poor condition. I could only imagine how many other men had resided in this very box or how long their stay was. This room was constructed to suppress any faith an inhabitant may have entered with. It snatched your beliefs of exterior possibilities. Only thing you were able to believe in was the time you had with yourself. Surrounded by nothing but yourself decreased the size of the room to the point of overcrowding. The capacity of the room was for one only, but every version of self comes alive: The Tough Guy, The Scary Kid, The Wrongfully Accused, and

the one you've been running away from for years—My Own Worst
Enemy.

  Their voices start to crescendo, getting louder, more distinct,
and utterly confusing. You can't determine which is the real "you."
Sanity is a lost art you become unfamiliar with. There's no escaping
it. You're quickly reminded this is all a part of who you are. Each
voice fueled by the thoughts, actions, and experiences of your past
that were never completely dealt with.

   The Tough Guy paces back and forth, pounding his
   right fist into the palm of his left hand. He then
   proceeds to readjust his pants as if preparing to
   fight. "Yo, I swear, I should of just swung at that
   big bear looking n*gga. It's a reason I'm in here, too.
   Imma take my respect," he yells.

   The Scary Kid just sits on the end of the bed with
   his head buried in his hands, catching the tears.
   "I just don't un…un…understand," he mumbles
   through the muted tears he lets out.

   The Wrongfully Accused stands on the wall adja-
   cent to the bed with his arms folded, not saying a
   word, shaking his head and displaying a concerned
   look on his face.

   My Own Worst Enemy also stands, but he faces
   everyone else with a smirk of disgust on his face.
   He expresses disapproval for everyone in the room
   with vigor in his voice. "Sit down! You ain't built
   for this jungle, so stop fronting and talking about
   what you should of did. You had the chance and
   what you do? Nut up. You ain't no better than this
   weak makeshift poor excuse of a man over here,
   praying his mommy comes to save the day," he vehemently responds to The Tough Guy as he points

and makes reference to The Scary Kid. "And you, Mr. Wrongfully Accused, you guilty just like every other animal up in here. Wake up, inhale the filth of this cage, and man up! Prepare yourselves for the glorious demise of the man in the mirror. There is no recovering from this, so embrace it. What's next is only worse. Facing that judge, who doesn't care anything about a black man, just ready to send another colored down the road for the most minuscule charge. Not to mention misrepresentation by some underpaid public defender more concerned with clearing his check than about your freedom. See, what y'all imbeciles are failing to realize is that even when freedom of the body comes, there's still entrapment of the mind. Only thing that changes is the address. This sh*t is over, and ya'll too sightless to see it," he concludes.

But I didn't quite understand the statement: *even with freedom of the body there's still entrapment of the mind.* How could I be trapped mentally if I was free from this place? I sat there attempting to drown them all out and focused on finding the meaning of that phrase. Before I could spend too much time pondering that idea, I heard a familiar voice and the unlocking of the deadbolt boxing me in. It was my mom. My stomach dropped. I had never been so thrilled to see my mother. Her irreplaceable smile caused the other cohabitants of my cage to vanish. I knew she was allowed in here only because of her affiliation with the sheriff's office and didn't have to go through the official visitation process.

"Hey, Boop, you okay?" she asked.

"Yes, ma'am. I'm making it," I replied, hiding the fact I was anxious to leave. I reflected back on all the times she was strong for me and omitted emotion in hard times, so I returned the favor. This wasn't the time to be weak in front of my mother no matter how much I desired to break down. She was going through more than her fair share of grief in her marriage, and now her son was behind the same walls she tried so hard to keep him away from.

"Your court date is set for tomorrow, and we're hoping you'll be released," she told me. But then it hit me. I would need a lawyer. An expense I knew we couldn't afford. Only viable option for me was a public defender. Then it hit me again. Just yesterday, I spent the entire Saturday with Jermaine and Ronald at Ronald's house, and his dad is a lawyer.

"Hey, mom, when you get home, look in my phone and call Ronald. His dad is a lawyer. See if he can help me," I said partially enthused, knowing I had no real guarantee. I figured he would remember me since I was just at his house less than 24 hours ago. *Funny how life worked out*, I thought. Going from laughing and joking with Ronald's father and now needing him to argue my freedom—all in less than a day.

"I'm not sure if he specializes in criminal law, but it's worth a try. Better than getting assigned a public defender," I concluded. She wrote the name down to remember to make this a priority when she returned home.

"How are you and Monica doing in all this?" I inquired. I was more concerned about their well-being than my own because inside this box I was safe, unlike them on the outside in reach of my stepfather. That worried me.

"Boop, we are both just fine. God got us. You stop worrying," she replied smiling. She knew me so well it wasn't even funny. No matter how old I got or how much of an adult I felt I was, I would still be her Boop.

As she left, she told me," Son, whether you know it or not, this is part of God's plan. Pray, asking him for clarity and how this situation will be for the betterment of you. I love you and will see you soon."

I didn't know what to do with her advice. There was no rational reason I could come to as to how imprisonment of my body was for my betterment. This situation was just another example of my doubt in God. Then My Own Worst Enemy reappeared. He sat right next to me and began mocking my mom's advice.

> So you're telling me it was God's plan to send you to this hell-hole? Or let me get this straight, you're here to learn a lesson about how to be passive-aggressive, allowing someone to kick your door in? Were you supposed to unlock the door for him and welcome him in? That is bullsh*t. You don't belong in here. It should be Curtis in here rotting in this box. If anything, you be asking God why?

> *Why, Lord, am I the imprisoned one?*
> *Why couldn't this graduation weekend be normal like everyone else's?*
> *Why do I need to be continuously tested in life?*

> Get those answers and maybe you'll achieve some clarity. Otherwise, what's the point? Ain't nobody coming to break you out anytime soon. You're subject to this justice system that's built to destroy black males.

All I could do was lie down and attempt to sleep. This was my gateway to freedom. As time elapsed, I would be even closer to getting out of jail. This was also a way of tuning out the influence of My Own Worst Enemy. His words began sinking into my ears, traveling to my brain, and collecting momentum in my thoughts. I had to combat these adverse thoughts because they would lead to destruction only.

I awoke to another knock on the exterior of the steel door to my box. It was the food crew delivering meals. Wiping my eyes and putting on my glasses, I reached over to retrieve the food tray. I was starving and ready to eat just about anything—until I looked over the contents of my meal. Food was too generous a description to label this slop fed to inmates. It was another indication of just how rough this place was.

Men are treated foully by correctional officers, malnourished with poor excuses for meals while fending for their lives against other inmates. How could anyone act sensibly in such conditions? But what voice did they have. They were outcasts of society, forever garnishing the label of the condemned. Some form of rehabilitation this was. I set the tray down on the floor, only drinking the packet of powered juice I mixed with water from the sink. Then I laid back down, hoping to fall into a much deeper sleep.

For hours, I tossed and turned on the cot. It felt like I was lying on the sidewalk, it was so hard. I wondered what time it was because there was no real way to tell. There was no indication if it was day or night. Then all of a sudden, I heard a deep male voice yell, "Lights out." Everything turned black. The only stream of light I got was from the 6" x 6" window overlooking the control panel, and even that was dimmed. I just wanted to sleep. I didn't want any more visitors—nothing but sleep. Freedom was just on the other side of one night's sleep. That's all I could think about—freedom when I got out.

Waking up to the sounds of yelling periodically throughout the night, rest didn't exist on the inside. It was non-stop restlessness tormenting your mind.

Air!
I need air!
I panicked.

I jumped off the bed, throwing up again. I was dry hurling nothing but the powder drink I had hours ago. I wasn't doing so well. Help wasn't coming, only more hours of darkness. Being alone never seemed so bad until this night. It was a horrible experience.

The next morning finally arrived at the turning on of lights and the opening of the food tray dropping off more slop. I just set it down on the floor and waited for a trustee to come back around to collect the tray. I knew my court appearance was approaching, only a few more hours I thought. I started to wonder if my mom was able to get hold of Mr. Langston, Ronald's father, to represent me before the judge. Only time would tell.

As the officers gathered the shackles to secure the inmates headed to court, I had never before been so excited to be bond by chains. I stood as the officer approached my holding cell, knowing the drill by placing my hands through the food tray slot for the handcuffs. Then proceeding to stand back as the door unlocked, holding on the officers instructions to step out to the line where inmates were determined "in" or "out" of bounds for the placing of the shackles.

I was then escorted to a holding room right behind the courtroom where inmates awaited their time with the judge to plead innocence or hear the fate of their guilt. Sitting in that back room, chained down to benches, everyone had stern looks on their face, maintaining their toughness and not giving off any signs of weakness. As the only offender present wearing the famed orange jumpsuit, I sat in silence, relying on the costume to incite fear into those around me. Then another orange jump-suited inmate was chained to my left. We looked one another right in the eye as if it were a staring contest. The first to look away was the loser, the weaker one. It was a psychological test of each other's manhood. My survival instincts kicked in, and surviving was the only objective. There was a chance I may see him again if this court appearance didn't go too well, so the tone had to be set. After he saw I wasn't going to give in, he eventually looked away. And before I could relish in the moment, I was summoned to stand before the judge.

Entering the courtroom, I immediately recognized a familiar face. Mr. Langston was there to defend me. Boy was I glad to see him. I was ashamed this was where we would meet again, not even 24 hours after being in the comfort of his home. He spoke with compassion, expressing to the judge that I was a stranger to trouble. In fact, this was my first run in with the law, and it was the result of domestic issues with my parents boiling out of hand. He continued to detail that I was a graduate of a prestigious high school and college bound in less than two months. "Judge, I ask that my client be released on his own recognizance." Meaning that I, the defendant, would adhere to attend all future court hearings or be found in contempt of the court.

The judge accepted his recommendation under strict guidelines that included having no contact with Curtis and that I not leave Duval county limits. She continued to assign me a parole officer with whom to check in, who would also verify that I completed the court mandated anger management courses in addition to community service at the Clara White Foundation. I thanked the judge and Mr. Langston, and then followed the court officer back to the jail where I would retrieve my things and be released.

I stood outside the walls of the jail for a second to take in the reality of my situation, not feeling any remorse for my actions. I did what I thought was right by protecting my family. It was just unfortunate the police didn't see it that way.

In the ensuing weeks, I completed all of the court ordered classes and visits with my assigned parole officer. My concern now was how to attend my college orientation, given the mandate to stay within county limits. My parole officer wasn't any help. All she did was push papers around, taking no interest in what my future held. I was scared that college was going to be a lost dream until I went to see Mr. Langston.

> Ismael, I honestly think you're a good kid, so I'm going to recommend to the judge that you be allowed to leave the county limits and attend your orientation. I just ask that you don't be like the rest of these jokers around here your age and actually do something with your life. Don't let me see you back in trouble. Get out of Jacksonville and make something of yourself.

I heard him loud and clear. I had no intentions of getting into any more trouble. His words were my ticket away from bondage—a ticket into a new life to do something none of the men I knew growing up ever could do, but a ticket away from the only family I had. In my eyes, life could only get worse by staying home, where complacency would consume my mind and every particle of my body and soul.

The thought of leaving my mom and sister in such turbulent times made me feel lower than a coward. *How could I be so selfish? What if someone breaks into the house?* But a better Ismael was what everyone needed. I was on my way to Orlando as a Golden Knight, never wanting to return to suffocate in Jacksonville.

EVEN CATER-PILLARS ONE DAY FLY

THE ENEMY: *You won't graduate college, no other man in your family has before. And trust me, you're no better than they are. You'll be right back in Jacksonville trapped mentally and physically. Obstacles of stress will block any plans of advancement. No one will be proud of you because you will fail them. Yes, you will fail... The complacency around you will take every last one of your breaths away, clouding your lungs with mediocrity. A dreamer who will die known as the Forgotten.*

MY FRESHMAN YEAR AT THE UNIVERSITY OF CENTRAL FLORIDA CAN BE DESCRIBED WITH ONE WORD: RECLUSE. I was far from outgoing, ignored strangers, and wasn't open to attending organizational meet and greets on campus. I steered clear of overly large social settings unless I knew at least one person attending. Usually, that one person was my dorm roommate, Marvin. He and I had known each other previously from high school, so it made the transition to college slightly easier.

Marvin was the polar opposite of me. He was a social butterfly just ready to spread his wings on campus. He was popular in high school from his involvement in chorus, to being the assistant student director, and blessed with the ability to play a variety of instruments. Before we graduated high school, we talked about being roommates and he had already mapped out all the organizations he planned on joining. One of them was Alpha Phi Alpha. I can remember drawing the undeniable parallels between joining a fraternity and joining a gang. "Marv, they both have colors and both are willing to fight if they see someone not a part of their organization wearing their colors or using their hand signs. And both push the security of brotherhood and community honor. How can you not see the similarities?" I concluded. This was an argument I was convinced I wouldn't lose, but to my ignorance of Greek-letter organizations, he calmly enlightened me.

"Ish, you are misinformed, man. Have you even researched Alpha or any other fraternities? Alpha has produced some of the most profound leaders in our community. Jesse Owens, Thurgood Marshall and a little-known Martin Luther King, Jr. Yeah, my good sir. You are highly misinformed. Some of the greatest earth shakers are Alpha men," he replied. I had no rebuttal and let the conversation go. There wasn't much for me to say because I didn't have much knowledge outside of my gang research.

Marvin continued his musical aspirations well into undergrad by joining the UCF Gospel Choir comprised by other psalmists ready to uplift their angelic voices unto the Lord. I had no interest in that area because I wasn't blessed with tonal structure. All my notes in high school chorus were off most of the time, so I just stayed to myself. I left my dorm room for only two main reasons, classes and food—or simply to walk around at night. I became quite the wanderer on campus. The university grounds resembled a mini resort with everything one could imagine right there. I wanted to discover all of its intricacies. At night, the hidden secrets of UCF were unveiled. The fountain at Millican Hall illuminated the five-floor library and surrounding areas. I soaked up every moment, thinking about how I almost didn't make it here. The campus was simply beautiful. All my other time was spent in Orange Hall of the Libra community, room 315. I played my Xbox 360 and seldom spoke when encountering unfamiliar faces.

I grew a new respect for Marvin during the course of our freshman year. He was wise far beyond his years and dealt with a lot of my demons on impact. I endured a period during my freshman year in which I contemplated leaving school because I was too far away from my mother and sister. Again, I was more concerned with their safety than my education. He even helped me to combat a cough syrup addiction.

I was struggling to sleep at night, allowing my mind to take over, worried about things far beyond my control—from parting ways with Brandy, my high school sweetheart, to overwhelming feelings of guilt for leaving Jacksonville, to going back to not speaking with my father. I was boiling over with emotion and didn't know how else to cure myself. One of my close friends from high school, Gerald, who was attending Tennessee State University in Nashville, called me one night, professing how he wanted to kill himself. I was speechless. The phone call was bizarre to say the least. "Hello," I said. He sounded like he was laughing, so I laughed, too. But I soon found out those weren't laughs, but screaming tears. I stopped in my tracks, praying that I didn't say the wrong words and causing him to ultimately kill himself. In the background, I could here yelling, "Gerald, please put the knife down." My heart sunk.

Why would he want to die?
Why did he call me?
What do I say?
What was he going through that was so bad that he didn't want to live anymore?

"Hey, man, talk to me. Just talk to me," I said. Gerald had explained to me that he'd been drinking excessively, trying to drown his problems, but he only amplified their prevalence in his life. He had opened the door to issues he had avoided dealing with for too long. He was imploding, and the liquor caused everything to just pour out. This was all too familiar to me and increased my dislike of liquor and those who partook in drinking. I'd seen it bring out the worst in people time after time. I couldn't understand the addiction. The consumption of alcohol seemed to ease the pain of people's realities, but I didn't see it that way. I scolded them all. And like the true hypocrite I was, I would drink my promethazine with codeine, running away from my very own issues.

I was prescribed the medication during my senior year of high school to combat chronic asthma. I was warned of the dangers by my doctor and especially cautioned on how addictive the substance could be.

"Ismael, I'm only giving you this to slow down the cough. This is not for you to abuse or share with your buddies. This prescription is very potent and nothing to mess around with. I'm only going to give you one refill on this and if you need any more from there, I'll be the one to examine your cough to determine if it's truly necessary," Dr. Emmanuel, my primary care doctor, said with a serious look on his face.

The bottle that I received in my freshman year was my one refill bottle. I ordered it behind my mother's back during the spring semester of 2010. I didn't want her interrogating me or worried that I was struggling with my asthma. Lying to my mother wasn't something I practiced or wanted to begin doing. So I figured if she didn't know, it was a nice work around. Every time I took it, I would increase the dosage. It got to the point where I wouldn't even look at the measuring cup, but drank the medication straight from the bottle. The side effects included severe drowsiness, blurred vision, weakness, tiredness, nausea, and vomiting. The normal dosage was enough to knock anyone out for the day, and upping the dosage would claim victory over my motor skills for days at a time. I found a safe haven within the contents of that bottle of medicated cough syrup. Life would slow down with each sip—my brain alleviated of my stress and minimized of my problems.

That thick, curvy, crimson-red liquid took care of me. It hid me from me. It never abandoned me, and it made me feel weightless. It was evident I was depressed by all clinical definitions, but too naïve to acknowledge it. But once the effects wore off, I would get blitzed by my issues all over again. The cough syrup didn't erase anything; it only prolonged my issues. Without taking it, I would become noticeably irritable and suffered severe stomach pains. In addition to an unhealthy diet of ramen noodles, pizza, and omelets from the local café, I was in a world of trouble.

Marvin noticed it had become problematic when I stopped showing up to our microeconomics class. Another problem indicator was when he returned from choir rehearsal at night, I would be in the same spot as when he left in the morning for classes. I had completely stopped attending classes. I just depended on classmates to pass me their notes. I would only show up on test days. I was completely losing sight of my purpose for attending college.

"Hey, bro. We need to talk," he began. "I know you got a lot up there on your mind, but you have not come this far to throw it all away. You're too smart and way stronger than this. I can't just sit back and watch you do this to yourself. You're no different than your grandfather or dad."

That was exactly what I didn't want to hear. That statement angered me, burning the interior of my eardrums.

I'm nothing like them.
I wasn't an alcoholic.
How could he fix his mouth to say such a thing?
Is he right?
Did I possess those same red eyes?
No, no, no!
Actually, I'm worse.
I'm an addict.

All I could do was nod my head in apparent shame and mumble, "You're right. I'll stop." I truly had intentions of stopping at the end of this bottle, of course. But IT had me, and there was no letting go. The taste was too sweet and the alluring feeling I couldn't give up.

I swear I just wanted to sleep, nothing more.
This was my cure to all my problems.
How could he not understand?
I don't even care anymore.

Marvin was solely expressing his concern as a friend, and someone who wanted what was best for me. I began going to class again and showing small improvements. I stopped for a few days, but the nights grew progressively longer. My insomnia was back. Lying in bed, tossing and turning for hours, the frustration would build. I could see Marvin sound asleep, just basking in the glory of sweet rest. I envied him as I looked at the bottle of cough syrup. So I collapsed back into the world of slow motion and endless lethargies. I just couldn't shake loose.

At the conclusion of the bottle's contents, I knew I couldn't get more without creating a commotion, so I moved down to Nyquil. It didn't pack the same punch, but it could get me to sleep. By this time, months had passed and Marvin was fed up.

"Ismael, I'm pouring all of them out right now. It's for your own good," he said with determination in his voice. It wasn't fair to him to be rooming with an addict, let alone one he knew well and saw so much potential in. I wasn't holding up my end as a roommate. Our living arrangements were uneasy, and it was my fault. I didn't add any positivity to the environment that was conducive to academic success or collegiate fun. I couldn't imagine the impact I was having on Marvin.

I allowed my problems to spill over into his daily life, and that wasn't fair. But my addiction didn't stop. To avoid any detection, I would pour the Nyquil into Gatorade bottles. I figured this way Marvin wouldn't know the difference. But I underestimated him because he did notice. I had a serious problem that required real help. Then Marvin beefed up his arsenal by threatening to call my mom, telling her what I was doing. I'd given him her number on moving in together, in case of an emergency. He was completely done and not bluffing. Marvin's poker face wasn't one you took lightly. He always meant what he said. He never wasted a word. I just couldn't break my mother's heart. His warning was more than enough. I thought about the disappointment I would cause. She had been through enough of late. I refused to let her see me like that. And not to mention my sister looked up to me, and I wasn't giving her much to admire. I had to get my life back on the right track. It took me almost a year and a half to fully kick the addiction, but I was glad the slump was over.

As a family, we had jus gotten past the violent altercation between my stepfather and me. Collectively, it took a great deal of time, but I wanted nothing more than for my mother to be happy. She deserved that much. I wasn't selfish enough to stand in the way of my mother's happiness. Never did I want her to have to choose between her child and her husband. That wasn't fair, especially when I wasn't going to be living at home again. Who was I to dictate what went on in their household? So Curtis and I buried the hatchet like men. It was never to be spoken about again, and we shook hands to not only co-exist but work towards establishing a relationship. I respected Curtis more than I ever managed to tell him.

From that point on, he loved my sister and me like his very own. Whenever we needed something, not once did he ever say no. It was admirable. If he was short or unable to deliver, he would present several options as solutions to obtaining what we were asking for. He was a man of his word, and I couldn't ask for more. I learned a lot from Curtis, post our fall out. He demonstrated what a work ethic was. The man took his job as a security consultant for Glass House Security Systems more than seriously. Succeeding in that role was just as important as his next heartbeat. I watched him pull 14-plus hour days just to reach the top of the sales list each month. He attended seminars where industry experts discussed trends and gave insightful advice on the future of technology in security. Driving around in the car, he listened to audio books on financial retention and the secrets to selling.

The man was unstoppable. He even had me passing out flyers to all the doors in our neighborhood—for a small fee, of course. Observing him made me look inward and challenge my own work ethic. I questioned my personal drive.

Am I putting in enough hours?
How do I measure up against competitors?
How do I get better?
What are the resources I need to tap into?
Am I making the right connections with people who can help me?

These were questions I knew the answers to. I was far from reaching my potential, and being as reserved as I was in my freshman year of college, it wasn't going to propel me anywhere. I had to rearrange my attitude towards relationship building and actually put in effort. I was ready for sophomore year. Marvin and I had moved off campus into our own respective apartments but with different roommates. Personally, I didn't blame him. Don't even think I ever apologized for exposing him to my addiction. But we remained in contact throughout the remainder of our undergrad years.

Living off campus in my own apartment was liberating. The overall cost was significantly cheaper than remaining on campus in student housing. More importantly, I had privacy. Having my own room and bathroom was more appreciated than having suite mates to share a shower and a roommate to share sleeping quarters. My apartment was far more spacious than anywhere I'd lived before. My new roommates were Jermaine, Malcolm, and Thomas. I knew them all from high school. Jermaine, my best friend, was entering his freshman year at Valencia Community College. Malcolm was in the same graduating class as Jermaine whom I didn't remember much from high school, but he seemed cool. He, too, was starting his freshman year at Valencia. Thomas was a year older than I and was entering his junior year in college. He was far more acclimated with the campus than the rest of us. Thomas played basketball in the recreation center a lot and had made a name for himself. Everyone was different in his own way, but we all got along without any problems. Our apartment was like one big man cave—and clean, I might add. I was overly compulsive about cleanliness, making it clear to my new roommates to uphold their parts in cleaning.

My second undergraduate year proved to be a turning point in my life. I began to evolve into an outgoing soul, free of the barriers that held me back previously. I wanted to make friends for a change and to actually enjoy myself. I made the decision to actually join student clubs on campus. After watching Curtis put in the time to achieve high accolades at work, I knew I had to step it up. I began attending club meetings on my own and through the recommendation of other students.

> *Maximize your exposure.*
> *The more organizations you join the better.*
> *But will this actually take me further?*
> *Will I fit in with the other members?*
> *What value will I add to the group's dynamic?*

One of the organizations I found of interest was Men of Integrity. It was a service-based organization focused on building up minority males by instilling the principles of leadership, community activeness, and self-sufficiency. The intent was to build character through social engagement. I really didn't know what I was searching for in an organization, but I was searching for some type of fulfillment. Another campus organization I grew fond of was the National Society of Black Engineers. As a civil engineering student at the time, I felt it was a no brainer. It simply made the most sense. But after a whole year of online reading and on-campus observation, I knew I wanted to become a member of the Xi Iota Chapter of Alpha Phi Alpha Fraternity, Incorporated.

During my freshman year, Marvin talked in great detail about the illustrious history of the organization, piquing my interest. I began conducting my own research on the fraternity's Founders, mission statement, and principles. I was blown away that I had never before heard of it. All of this black history was hidden from me, and no one in my family had gone to college let alone been a member of a black Greek-letter organization. Therefore, it was understandable how I missed it. Marvin exposed me to Alpha, and for that I am grateful. But I wanted to know more than the Internet had revealed.

I wanted to know how to become an actual member, and I knew exactly who to ask—my main man Kendrick.

Talk about having the *juice* on campus or being the cool kid. Kendrick had it all. From holding leadership roles to being surrounded by attractive women every time I saw him—the brother was winning. I felt comfortable talking to him about anything because we had years of friendship under our belts. But when asking about Alpha, he offered absolutely no preferential treatment. At that point, I knew it had to be earned.

Kendrick and I met back in 2005 in high school at basketball tryouts. As a freshman, I was the humble tryout just looking to fill a spot on junior varsity, nothing more. He was trying out for the varsity team along with Terrance. Both were juniors with a bit of experience on their side and clout as returning players. In the conditioning portion of tryouts, I got my first taste of each of their personalities. The two of them were so different but alike in many ways.

Kendrick was a unifier of people through his outgoing yet inclusive personality. He didn't know what the word *stranger* meant. It was a non-existent concept to him. The man could make friends with foreigners, speaking in their native tongue. It was his gift. Dottie, as he was commonly known, was super ambitious, reaching past the stars in his endeavors. Being the youngest of three brothers, he'd accumulated a lot of life experiences from his two older siblings. They showed him their wins and losses in life, better preparing him for how he should handle situations. It gave Kendrick an edge in life while he set his own high precedents for achieving. He was an honor-roll student and part-time rapper, whose claim to fame came in the rap group named F.T.G. (Full Time Grind) with their leading single, *Get It Wet*. The mega group consisted of Dottie and Darrin aka Wattz. Dottie loved music, just the way I did. It was a prominent component of our friendship. Both of us were able to listen far beyond the musical elements of songs, hearing the vulnerability in the delivery of an artist. Dottie was the big brother I never had.

He provided me with advice on life in the same way I'm sure his brothers did with him. His opinion mattered to me because of the respect and admiration I had for him. Dottie was one of the few people in the world whom I could share my stories with, no matter whether good or bad. When I was wrong, he never held back in telling me.

"Dawg, you are tripping," he once began. "The way you handled that situation wasn't right, but it's still reconcilable only if you can put your pride aside." I trusted him to lead me down the correct path. Not only did he challenge my wrongs, he also provided sound advice for how to make amends in each situation.

Terrance, on the other hand, was the apprehensive one when it came to including "outsiders." And he didn't mind making you feel out of place. He was full of smart remarks in which you were usually the butt of the joke. He was a misunderstood soul. On the surface—let me be honest—he was an asshole. But once you got to know him, he'd impress you with his depth of knowledge. Terrance could speak on foreign policy, products affecting the ozone that caused global warming, and other topics your average 17-year-old was clueless about. He was a hungry reader who valued the possibilities of words while fulfilling his appetite for information. He inspired me to read at a time in my teenage life when I thought it was uncool. Terrance was also another child prodigy and honor-roll student who had the support of his teachers. They loved him. It amazed me how easily he could turn on and off his use of slang and street dialogue to converse with school administrators.

Terrance was a logical thinker who viewed each situation holistically. His careful decision-making allowed him to weigh all consequences of a given decision. In his everyday conversations, he demonstrated his ability to provide perspectives C through Z when a given conversation called for A and B only. From him I was able to share experiences and get various unexplored options as feedback. He rarely agreed with my thinking, but I wasn't sensitive enough to take offense to it. I can't lie, though. I treaded carefully when approaching him with anything because I knew he was going to go somewhere else with it. I needed Terrance in my life for that very reason.

Kendrick and Terrance complimented each other like Will Smith and Martin Lawrence's characters Mike Lawry and Marcus Burnett in the "Bad Boys" movie series. They joked on each other with no remorse. They were hilarious. The two of them took yo momma jokes to a whole new level. Nothing was off limits between them, which truly showed the camaraderie they shared. And my absolute favorite thing about them was their constant stuttering. Not because they couldn't speak fluidly, but because their minds processed faster than their tongue could handle. They sounded like two drunk fools. Everyone around them picked on their speech "impediment."

Kendrick and Terrance would continue their bond into college and further into Alpha. They were dudes who I looked up to since high school, and I wanted to share in that fraternal bond with them. Outside of them, my interest was further piqued when looking on campus and wondering where the Alphas were. They were never on the scene, not even on Black Wednesday, the Greek-designated day to wear jerseys and other Greek organizations' paraphernalia. I was beyond curious as to why they weren't visible.

My answer would come at an informational, at which all the current Chapter members of Xi Iota introduced themselves by name and the leadership positions they held on campus. I was blown away. I was exposed to a collective of young black males shattering stereotypes of what America said we should be. They were well spoken, dedicated to academic excellence, and the empowerment of their Chapter's members. I was in dire need of professional and personal development, so I knew they could help me in both areas. After hearing the accomplishments of other potential initiates and what they had to offer the Chapter, I didn't feel I belonged. I had nothing to bring to the organization. But if they granted me the opportunity to join, I would work circles around each and every one of them to prove my worth. I held no executive board positions and didn't have the highest of grade point averages—just a strong determination to prove to them that I was worthy of selection.

At 12:36am on December 3rd in the fall of 2010, I officially became the newest member of the house of Alpha—never looking back to dwell on the person I was before. I was tired, fatigued, and overjoyed. No other feelings could compare. The words *I*, *me*, and *mine* no longer existed; they were words that did not rhyme. The words *we*, *us*, *ours*, *together* were substituted, words that would last forever. Lessons learned on this journey—with my line brothers Barnell Warren, Jonathan Baucom, Joel Joseph, Zumarr Archer, and Evan Easterling—would mold us into men our communities, families, and friends would not recognize. We were now men of manly deeds, scholarship, and expressors of love for all mankind. To say I'm thankful for them would be an understatement. Being the youngest in this brigade of men, I was able to learn and empower myself through their teachings of life. I turned my eyes to them for strength, motivation, and for the blueprint of manhood because I was still searching. We were six individuals, living completely separate lives, not involving one another—but transforming together into one unbreakable yolk.

We laughed together, cried together, and withstood the darkest of times—together. We were brothers. Born of different parents but united by loyalty. Like all true siblings, we had disagreements—yelling and cursing to the boiling point that, sometimes, turned into physical altercations. Nothing was done out of malice or ill intent, but we vowed to resolve all issues internally, never allowing anything to penetrate our nucleus.

Barnell was the overly hyper man-child with muscles who never really grew up. He found joy in aggravating me. Whether it was by picking at my gap, saying how stupid I was, or just looking at me for far too long—he and I fought the most. On one particular occasion, we got into it at his family reunion, just before we had to perform a step for his kinfolk. As much as we fought each other, we always ended in breathless laughs. It took us a while to regain our wind because we'd really go at it while our other line brothers looked on laughing. At the end of the day with Barnell, I knew I could always go to him for a laugh. The dude was the world's funniest undiscovered comedian. His stories would be so elaborate in detail it didn't matter whether he was lying or not; they were tearjerkers.

Jonathan was one of the older, more involved members of our line. He was truthfully one of two of us who actually represented what I thought an Alpha was—eloquent in his speech, polished in his appearance, a resume full of credentials. If anyone deserved Alpha, it was he. As a proud member of Alpha Kappa Psi, the Professional Business Fraternity, he got joked on often by all of us for his deep love for his business frat. We gave him hell. But Jonathan moved to the beat of his own drum, which is what I respected about him.

Joel, or JJ as we called him, was the man on campus. Whether you knew him or not, he needed no introduction. He made it a point to befriend every person he came in contact with. His energy was infectious—or annoying, depending on the person. JJ was a man of many hats. He was student director of the Campus Activities Board, in which he oversaw a half-million dollar budget to fund concerts, Late Knights, and other fun student activities. At the same time, he worked for the Orlando Magic as a guest servicer. Oh, and did I mention he had a 3.9 grade point average? No task was too big or small for JJ. He flourished under pressure, making 16-hour days look like a breeze. He showed me the importance of being involved on campus, and he represented what it meant to be a model student. The dude wasn't someone I would have hung out with prior to Alpha, but man did I love him for being so fearless.

Zumarr was the oldest of our line and the most humble person you'd ever meet. He operated in the background, to a high degree at that. Ladies loved Cool Zumarr. His meekness was admirable. As a former collegiate wrestler, he was built like Randy "Macho

Man" Savage. He would often find himself falling victim to Barnell and my jokes at times. I soon stopped after he threatened to rip out my spine through my rectum. At that point, I figured it was in my best interest to scale it back or tell the joke at a distance, safe enough to get out of his reach because if he grabbed me—life was over. Did I mention his sense of humor? Oh, man, Zumarr had one of the most interesting senses of humor. It was borderline weird, but it worked for his reserved personality. "Hey, Ish, your feet look like a pack of wild wolves...ha ha ha." This was his most infamous crack on me because when he told it, no one laughed. Everyone just sat, confused, like what in the hell are you talking about. Was it funny? Yeah, it was, but his delivery just blew it, especially after telling it after Barnell had been roasting me for the last 20 minutes.

Evan was the one always smiling, even after calling you a female dog. His sarcasm was second to none. One could never decipher what was real and what wasn't. Evan and I clicked instantly. He was a likeable dude who thrived on calling me out on my bull. I was infamous for embellishing stories and, boy oh boy, he would bring down the hammer. "Boy, stop lying. We know you ain't getting no chicks. You too ugly," or "Really, bruh? I know you lying," he would remind me all too often. He questioned every story I told, which kept me sharp because he made sure to call me on my foolishness. Evan had a big heart, he was the glue of our line, the one who made sure everyone was still breathing no matter how busy life became.

I wouldn't trade in these guys for anything in this world. They all have a special place in my heart. For them, I'll always be there until I'm called home by God himself. If they ever needed anything, I would give it to them, without a second thought. If they had kids, I'd treat them as if they were my own, making sure they wanted for nothing in life. Being so different is what made us so close; we had so much to learn about one another. Each of us represented a peculiar puzzle piece that fit together to create a masterpiece, and all it took was a little bit of S.A.C.R.I.Phice.

In addition to the lessons learned from my line brothers, one more influential man entered my life. John Ellis, Jr., Esq. was a mentor, friend, brother, and father figure. These were just a few of the hats John Ellis, Jr. wore in my life. He was the first man whom I wanted to be like. John was the man I needed to see in order to become a man myself—from the time we first met in the Fall of 2009 at an Alpha informational on campus to the time he took me under his wing as the Assistant District Director (ADD) of the Florida Federation of Alpha Chapters in October of 2011. I knew he could help me unlock the leader from within.

Serving as the District Director (DD) of the state of Florida and residing in the Orlando area, we began spending a lot of time together. As the newly elected ADD, I didn't know what was expected of me. I just knew I was an aid to the DD. John had it all prepared for me. He empowered me like no other person outside of my mother had before. "Brother Brown, you are more than a college brother. You are the voice of the college, brother. An active liaison communicating the grievances of your comrades. You are a beacon of hope for your community as a black leader. You are a representative of the greatest district in Alpha once you sit before fellow board members. You are an Alpha man and don't you ever forget it. Your responsibilities are greater and the burden is heavier as an Alpha," he finished. The man was a lawyer by trade, and it was evident in his dialogue. He was skilled in motivating people through his choice words.

Brother Ellis set a high bar for me to aim for and achieve as a man. A good majority of the time, I figured I'd never reach the zenith of manhood he put before me. It appeared too far out of reach. Talking with such an extensive vocabulary, walking with purpose, dressing for where you want to be and not where you currently are—I had a lot to learn. I thought I would have to approach these things alone, but John was there every step of the way. Communication for him was pivotal to the effectiveness of leadership; he took it very seriously. Brother Ellis would call me at least 2–3 times per day.

At the end of each call, we had a to-do list for me that got longer by the call. I thought to screen him a couple of times, but his voicemails were even longer.

I tried to minimize my role by being a position holder and not an upholder of the role. This was something he preached to me. "Brother Brown, as a leader, you must earn the respect of your followers daily. You are only as strong to them as they are to you. The relationship is a two-way street, but don't underestimate the misfortunes of leadership. Not everyone will support your initiatives, be present when you need them, nor will everyone comprehend your vision. It's on you to be able to persevere through all unexpected challenges. A great leader is not defined by his likeability but by his ability to impact lives."

I felt the things he was asking me to do were too much to carry along with trying to sustain a life. I wanted to be a leader without the work. He wouldn't allow me to be lazy or to fail in my role. He pushed me beyond what I thought I was capable of. His "never good enough" philosophy stressed me out. The pressure of not living up to his expectations scared me. My every move was ridiculed. Earning his satisfaction seemed less obtainable than winning Power Ball.

Over the course of the 2011–2012 fraternal year, he and I traveled all over the southern region attending other state conventions. We road tripped to Columbia, South Carolina; Macon, Georgia; and Orangeburg, South Carolina. Brother Ellis understood the importance of keeping up appearances, especially in the vast land of Alpha. You never knew what support you could garner that you would need one day. He also wanted to expose me to brothers outside of the state of Florida. "Alpha is bigger than Orlando. It's bigger than Florida. You have to be willing to travel to meet brothers where they are in order to expand your network. You don't know how they can help you. Brothers are endless resources; maximize these opportunities."

The road trips were fun, at least the parts that I was awake to enjoy. He would pick on me amongst other brothers, saying how I wasn't any good having him drive the whole way while I fell asleep on him. We all laughed, but I never took it to heart because Brother Ellis meant well. Honestly, I didn't sleep the whole way. He and I would talk strategy. He would allow me to lead the conversation as a way to hear my ideas and understand my thought process behind my ideas.

He actively listened and chimed in with feedback. "Brother Brown, that's a good idea to institute a seminar on transitioning from collegiate chapters to alumni. I believe it should be reinforced at Neophyte training," he responded. By providing direction and names of brothers to contact who could assist me, he gave me the confidence every leader needs to succeed. These long road trips were worth every minute because it was my chance to soak up the wisdom Brother Ellis had accrued over time. I still, to this day, couldn't tell you how old he is, but his lessons are timeless, bridging our age difference. By sharing the stories of his youth and of his one-time failed marriage, he opened the door for me to open up about my own life.

He shared with me where he'd made mistakes in life, along with ways he should have better managed each. Brother Ellis even smiled about some of his failures. I wasn't sure why. I just assumed maybe he felt good about saving me from repeating the same mistakes. "Brother Brown, you have to be able to look yourself in the mirror every day. If your decisions are obstructing your view of you, then you must realign your thinking," he said. The relevancy of his message was mind blowing. It was like he knew I struggled with my own image of self. It was like he was in my mind, or he had also experienced complications as a 21-year-old.

"Brother Brown, I'm going to tell you something else you may not be aware of. Women are by far more intelligent than we are. They are detail oriented, have an exquisite memory that allows them to notice our many routines, and they have the propensity to forgive but not forget." I responded with laughter at the idea that women were smart first and foremost. All the game I was running on a couple of girls at the time—I was yet to be caught or have any close run-ins.

> *Smarter?*
> *No, not at all.*
> *I'm around here switching the scene and role per night.*
> *If they were so smart, how come it was so easy for me to lie and evade any commitment?*
> *Naw, I was smarter.*

These were gems I let in one ear and out the other. I wasn't interested in the desires of no woman's heart, only my own and about what made me feel good. Anything outside of personal gain wasn't my concern. Little did I know how inexperienced I was and how listening to Brother Ellis could have helped me later because he was actually right.

"Another thing I'll tell you is to stop chasing trophies who can't offer you anything outside of their beauty. Brother Brown, looks are fleeting. After awhile you start to realize the thirst for someone else—someone who can mentally stimulate you, cook, and basically do everything besides appeal to your eye and flesh. You become bored quicker, therefore, inciting that feeling to hunt again. Find someone who can challenge you mentally all while supporting you in your endeavors," he concluded. I heard him, but again, I didn't listen. I was too far gone on being the Playa of the Year. Most of the men I've ever conversed with were promoting my misogynistic ways. Constantly reinforcing that validity from them came with the number of chicks I'd had sex with or the juggling act of maintaining a roster of options. Brother Ellis' advice didn't have a chance.

John Ellis, Jr. further propelled me into the ranks of Alpha by suggesting I put my name in the race for Assistant Regional Vice President. This was the highest position a collegiate brother could hold as a sitting board of directors member for the entire organization. The responsibilities were far greater than those of ADD. This position oversaw the entire Southern region, including seven districts (states): Alabama, Florida, Georgia, Mississippi, North Carolina, South Carolina and Tennessee. So that meant traveling to all seven state conferences, giving a state of the region address, coordinating a college brothers retreat, traveling to board of directors' meetings, and other special Alpha sponsored events. And these were only the surface-level tasks that could be discussed with candidates. The time constraints would be immense but not for the socially inclined.

At first I was uncertain because I was coming to the close of my college years and anxious to get out of school before accumulating any more student loan debt. Traveling so much with Alpha prevented me from securing any type of real job at the time, so I was putting myself in a bind financially by holding office. But at the same time, I didn't have a job lined up if I decided to graduate in the Fall of 2013. I expressed my concerns with Brother Ellis, but I was nervous because I knew he wanted this for me. But after careful consideration, I saw the value of adding this position to my resume would only appeal to employers and allow me to meet more people.

I had grown so much from the person who started college as a loner and now I was campaigning across the country soliciting votes and campaign funds. I could see the progression as a result of being mentored by someone I respected. He had my best interest at heart and I trusted him.

After months of campaigning, showing face at chapter meetings, and creating a platform to run on, the battleground was set at the 2013 Southern Region Convention in Mobile, Alabama. The stakes were extremely high. A record-high five candidates were vying after the seat. I didn't feel anything but tired. The semester had been a rough one academically. I was taking some of the tougher upper-level classes in my major. But there was no time to rest or relax for this weekend was bound to be a sleepless one. Brother Ellis assembled me a full campaign team comprised of undergraduate and alumni brothers. He had each of them assigned to positions to occupy outside of fraternal meetings with rotating schedules.

"Now, Brother Brown, you need to be out and about talking to everyone," he instructed me like a football coach strategizing for the Super Bowl. It was clear he had done this many times before. The brother didn't even sweat. On the other hand, I was nervous running against the many other polished candidates. Some of them already looked the part, but I refused to lose. The backbone of my campaign team consisted of the Xi Iota Spring 2013 neophytes. As their Dean, we had our times of disgust for one another, but our respect trumped personal feelings. I was, however, unsuccessful in communicating and managing expectations with them. I pushed them beyond their limits too soon. My vision was they would be the most elite Alphas to ever come through Xi Iota. The method to my madness completely failed to translate how much I cared for their development as men. I rarely if at all complimented their efforts for anything, only pointing out where they needed improvement. As a leader, I failed them. I didn't give them any constructive feedback, only comments destroying their progression. But without their dedication and support during that election, I had no way of winning.

Yes, I pulled off the victory—by a landslide at that, with my Inspire campaign composed of three tiers: opportunity, innovation, and change. I eloquently addressed three areas of need within our region, which impacted both undergraduate and alumni members. It was my full intent not just to close the gap, but to eliminate the gap between members. With Opportunity, I proposed the No Brother Left Behind Act, which called for a region-wide career fair in which each District would be held responsible for enlisting a preset number of hiring companies. This portion of the campaign also called for the pairing of professionals with collegiate members in associated majors. I figured this would, in natural order, develop mentorships amongst members.

The Innovation plateau promoted the spirit of entrepreneurship, implementing a new competition to allow brothers to present business plans and present their ideas for monetary rewards. I understood the power of investing within our own community in addition to the magnificent of ideas produced by the black community. It was an easy sell. When it came to the Change component, I intended to instill accountability amongst my college brothers by implementing bi-weekly grade reports. These reports would allow chapters to monitor members' academic performance. In return, it would also assist members with building rapport with professors for those times when letters of recommendation are needed or to strategically network with academia in their respective fields. I believed the impact of my Inspire campaign could not only do more for our members beyond the fraternity, but also instill life values in our brothers.

Brother Ellis was the first to come over to congratulate me. He was smiling like he had just won the lottery. The man was ecstatic. I smiled back knowing I made him so proud. That feeling was irreplaceable. Looking back over the last two years of our relationship, our bond felt stronger than that of fraternity brothers or mentor and mentee; he was a true father figure to me.

Brother Ellis' saw had sharpened the dull blade of Ismael and turned me into the sharpest sure-fire knife in the drawer. Whenever I was without anything, he dug down into his pocket and gave it to me. I remember being asked to attend a tuxedo-attired ball on behalf of the district of Florida one year, but I didn't own one. After telling him this, he chewed me out from A to Z, taking his time to explain how it was imperative that every man own a tux. "Brother Brown, meet me at K&G off Hiawassee and Colonial when you get out of class. This is pathetic," he ordered.

He invested into my development by purchasing my first black tux. "Brother Brown, you're going to look good when you go out into the world. I refuse to have you looking fickle, no sir, not on my behalf." I couldn't understand why he cared so much about me or what I had done to earn his support. I wasn't accustomed to a man dedicating so much time and effort into my progress. By nature, I wanted to reject it because this was so foreign to me. Running away from what I needed was what I'd always done, but pushing him away was impossible; he'd come running right after me.

It was that same tux I would wear at the General Convention in 2013 in Austin, Texas, where both my mother and Brother Ellis would attend. They were there to watch me take an oath to uphold the aims of Alpha Phi Alpha, leading the organization to new heights and earth-shaking historical moments. Reflecting back on life as the three of us posed for a photograph, I thought about how in the beginning as a child it was her love then and how now it was his wisdom that led me to this unforgettable moment. It couldn't have been done without them both.

Brother Ellis deserved a more forthcoming mentee. Not sure if he knows this or not, but he was the father figure I'd always wanted. Words can't describe the appreciation I have for him. Without his guidance, I'm 100 percent positive I would today be a poor excuse for an Alpha and an even worse man. Having a mentor who was someone I respected as a true role model meant all the difference in my life. I can only imagine the ignorance or stupidity I would have put forth without his high expectations and direction.

DEAR DAD,
I FAILED YOU

THE ENEMY: *Nobody's sperm donor was there for them. It's completely normal to have an absent father in the home. That's a part of the African American foundational discord. You all lack the cohesiveness of having support from both parents and, in turn, build up hatred for his shortcomings. No time to feel sorry for yourself nor hold your head down. You must rely on self to become the man he couldn't be to you.*

THIS CHAPTER WAS BY FAR THE MOST DIFFICULT CHAPTER TO WRITE. I skipped around to others, purposely avoiding this topic. However, it was necessary that I take my time with every word I detail about the relationship between my father and me. For months, I would find myself questioning what angle would I take in discussing the consanguinity we shared. I was mentally plagued with thoughts of regret—the regret that I could never fully know who I was or why I responded to certain situations if

I never took the time to ask my father who he was. You see, self-discovery is contingent on one's biological make up. My regret was rooted in the thought that I would ultimately wait until it was too late to reach out to my father. My fear was he would pass away, and I would live on with an enlarged heart, heavy with *un*forgiveness.

> *Did he deserve to lose a living son?*
> *Did I deserve to never know who I really was?*

Still to this day, I haven't been able to pick up that phone and reconcile things with my father. Am I scared of the fault I'd have to accept for the rift in our relationship after so many years? Or is it the feeing that I don't need him because I never felt like I ever had him? Or could it be the brutal reality setting in that I'm no different than someone whom I spent the majority of my youth despising? In actuality, it was a combination of all those things accompanied by being afraid that I did not know what to say or even how to approach the conversation. "Hey, dad, why are we mad at each other again? Why didn't we go to basketball games together? Why didn't you and mom work out your relationship?" The list of inaugural questions could go on for pages, but I never had faith in the idea that conversation could even be possible.

For years I found myself attempting to make amends with no success. It only further damaged the frail state we were in. I am by no means writing this chapter to demonize my father or his character, but I'm just expressing my thoughts towards my childhood and how his inconsistency of being in my life affected me well into my adulthood. Furthermore, this chapter will serve as the communication channel I use to reach out to my father. I will say everything here that I longed to tell him in person. I pray that our story inspires some young boy or girl or even an adult fed up with how things are between him or her and that parent. I can attest to just how important it is to reconcile with a parent you've longed to have in your life. It'll release the resentment you've locked away in your heart, unearth the roots of your unforgiving spirit, and free you from drowning in the depths of the sea of self-identity crisis.

*****

Dad, I want to start off by saying, "I forgive you." I've come to a point in life as a man in his twenties in which I realize I had to achieve a deeper level of understanding in order to place myself in your shoes. I would find myself thinking less of you because you were not the man I wanted you to be. Through my observations of other families—whether of my peers or on television—I manufactured this ideal version of what I desired in you. The picture perfect dad who would take me camping, teach me to play and love the sports you did as a child, teach me how to treat a woman, how to educate myself and, most importantly, how to be a superhero.

The superhero who possessed the super strength to carry the weight of his household on his back, lifting the responsibility off his wife to be, who would be able to fly high, soaring gracefully into the heavens where the blueprints of his dreams were outlined by the brightest of stars, who had the ability to save the day when his son and daughter let their eyes fill with tears from a long list of unfortunate situations that could be simply categorized as growing pains. The superhero who thoroughly enjoyed being the first responder to any sign of unstableness within the household. The ultimate superhero who's able to use his vulnerability to his advantage, showing his family his imperfections and allowing them to witness transformational growth.

Dad, these were the qualities I required of you and wanted to learn from you my entire life. Without these lessons, I truly felt incompetent and insecure in my decision-making abilities when it came time to prove my manhood. These situations covered all areas of my life—from poor financial choices to my inability to love anyone, including myself.

The desire to have a male influence and his approval and guidance was desperately needed. I was crying out for those intangibles, screaming on the inside for you to take my hand and guide me through the maze of manhood. I will not disrespect you by saying you were absent because that would be false and an unforgivable accusation. However, we have never had any consistency in our relationship, especially since the death of Papa. His untimely death shook the core of everything you and I ever knew. Larry Brown, Sr. was the most influential man in both of our lives—from that time to this very day. By examining everything we've been through, I have come to the conclusion that Papa is the greatest catalyst between us.

You see, Dad, I never told you this, but when Papa died, I promise it felt like I lost you both. Papa took a piece of you with him, leaving you incomplete. You grew distant, lost in a place of seclusion where words couldn't leave your lips without tears slowly following. I remember the day of his wake, after everyone left from viewing the body, you just sat in the room where the casket was with your head in your hands, vehemently crying. This was the result of holding it in when the family gathered. Every salutation was a reminder of the lost "Hey, Lil Larry" Dad. I just wanted to save you! I ran over to where you were sitting and just hugged you. I didn't want to let go because I knew just how much you needed it. That hug was the most genuine outward expression of love that you and I ever shared through the course of our years together.

Dad, I watched you devolve into a black empty abyss, looking to fill the void with any and everything you could find to soften the beating you were taking. Maybe you didn't realize it, but I could see you sniff coke lines through dollar bills, witnessing the evolution of your deep intoxications. Dad, it seemed like the drinking wasn't enough; guess you needed something stronger. I guess that void could only be filled by cocaine. As child, I didn't know the severity of your addictions. All I knew was your eyes matched Papa's. Those eyes were a reminder of the pain we just endured together in our own separate ways with no communication as to why or what happened. Dad, looking back on everything, I wish we had just talked about the problems Papa faced with alcoholism, and how that sickness affected you.

At the time, all I could fathom was that my grandfather drank himself to death, and I despised everyone who partook in the fiery taste of alcohol. As my friends raised shots towards the sky in celebratory occasions, or as mixed drinks were ordered by the rounds for mere enjoyment, I found myself drowning in a sea of anxiety. The uneasiness would arise from a place I attempted to suppress from memory—the thought of losing someone else close to me to alcohol. The anxiety would transform into something far worse. I became judgmental and condescending as I looked at people drink themselves into euphoric states.

> *Do you know what that stuff can do to you?*
> *Why participate in something that makes you less aware of your actions?*
> *How could you be so stupid?*
> *These fools won't even remember what happened tonight.*

These incidents with alcohol and drugs use would go on to deeply affect my outlook on life, causing me to distance myself from those who did drink. Dad, you were no different and that caused our great divide. We became more strangers than family. But guess what, Dad? The apple didn't fall too far from the tree. As I judged you, I became a hypocrite who was heavily inebriated from my own bottle of egoistical ways, and it made me sick. Yes, sick of you and sick of seeing you drink until you were incoherent. I was 7, you 27—both of us fatherless.

Being so young and naïve, I just knew you would stop drinking alcohol after you saw what happened to Papa. But you didn't. In fact, you drank more and your eyes began to look the same way as Papa's looked every time I saw him—dilated and bloodshot red. I remember looking through Granny's old family photos, and in all of them Papa had this look on his face as if he didn't know where he was—those same red eyes. Then I would ask you why he looked this way and you replied, "He's been drinking."

So, why dad?
Why follow the same blueprint of destruction for your own life?
Did you not care how I felt?
Did I not matter to you?
Were you ready to die?

Papa was an amazing man from what I can remember. He wasn't an angry drunk or one who became overly aggressive. His heart actually shined through the darkness of his drunkenness. He would give all he had. Dad, I hated watching you drink because I didn't want you to die, too. Losing Papa really had a tremendous affect on our whole family. I had never seen Granny cry so much, or you and auntie fight like cross-town enemies. I was witness to the annihilation of the Brown family.

By distancing myself from you, I took away your opportunities to teach me anything beneficial to my growth as a boy who would need these lessons as I became a man. Not once have I ever accepted ownership in our precarious relationship. I just commissioned all the blame to you. My entire mindset was cemented on the idea that my life was hard because of you. The lack of consistency among us is a prime example of my stubbornness and ability to hinder my own progression.

Dad, I remember in high school when mom couldn't afford my senior pictures, class ring, or yearbook; I saw the frustration on her face, telling me, "Son, I don't have it. I just don't have the money." I absorbed her frustration and mutated it into animosity aimed at no one else but you. All I wanted was some help to alleviate the stress off her shoulders and for you to be that provider I knew a man should be for his child. Although I have yet to have children of my own, I've known you both were equally responsible for making and raising me. "I'm just going to have to put in for some overtime. Don't worry. You haven't gone without anything this far, so let momma figure it out," my mom reassured me. But I couldn't bear to watch her kill herself for me. Dad, I had too much pride to watch her do that. In my mind, I should have been able to take care of myself and hold my own even at 17 because that was the type of pressure I placed on myself. So I got a job against the wishes of you both.

"Son, why are you in such a damn hurry to work? You ain't got no bills. Man, you got your whole life to go punch a clock," you told me sternly. But by that time there was nothing you personally could tell me to change my mind. To be honest, Dad, I didn't listen to any of your advice around this time. It fell on deaf ears. I felt that since you had no real hand in taking care of me, then why should I listen to you? I was working against you, and I'm sure I never detailed the severity of our financial situation to you anyway. Were we in danger of being evicted or going hungry? No, but we had no excess of funds for all of the expenses of my senior year in high school. I felt it was obvious we had a demand for money if I expressed my interest in finding a part time job. Nothing in me understood why you were so opposed to me gaining some responsibility, especially when you weren't providing. Yet once again, I proved to show how inefficient my communication skills were. I worked on the assumption you knew these expenses required your help, but not once did I ask you for anything.

I found myself carrying this same rage towards you well into my undergraduate years in college. I remember during my freshman year when my meal plan ran out and my mom had nothing to send me. She also had my sister to fend for. So I convinced myself I couldn't keep depending on her. Being the first to go to college, this was a true trial run. None of us knew how expensive school could really be.

Dad, in order to survive, I had to max out on student loans to cover tuition, housing, and then rent when I moved off campus. I had to survive, and that's all that mattered to me, knowing at some point these loans would cripple my adulthood.

Back in 2012, I was living in non-student apartments and loving my place. It was away from campus and really secluded. Jermaine and I had our own rooms, bathrooms, and walk-in closets. I couldn't have asked for anything more. I can vividly remember asking my mom to just front me rent money in January just until financial aid dropped, but she couldn't. How could I be mad at her, though? She had over extended herself time after time to help me. Dad, situations like this arose more frequently the older I got.

Internally, my disdain shifted from you to the man in the mirror. The two of us were like Frank and Jesse James, two wild outlaws pledged to incite carnage on all of our victims through theft and death. Hand-in-hand we generated hurdle after hurdle, making my life more difficult. The time had come for me to finally accept the role I had in my shortcomings and become aggressive in transforming my mindset, focusing on making the necessary amendments to my thinking. One's mind has the ability to create peace amongst warring countries; or in contrast, the power to spread hate through choice words followed by executed actions fueled by evil thoughts. So by taking an introspective look, Dad, I began to realize where I could help myself.

As a child, how could I have known the pressure you were under as a first-time parent, young adult, and fatherless yourself? It wasn't fair for me to apply additional pressure with my judgmental views. I did not know anything about managing relationships, balancing youth with responsibility, or raising a child. I was overly critical of your every move. As I got older, my criticism grew harsher with each passing year. Out of my own ignorance, I assumed things would improve without the communication of my grievances. I waited, and waited, and as no surprise, nothing changed. Things just progressively got worse.

My love for you never waivered nor was it ever in question. I remember the time when Magic and I came over to Granny's house, and we sat in the backyard talking for hours. You and Magic enjoyed each other's company. The both of you shared common interests in my development. Every time the two of you were together, it was nothing but laughs and stories about people or things foreign to me as a boy. But realistically, it never bothered me because I was just thrilled to be around the both of you. I would find myself forcing myself to laugh when you two laughed, just so I could seem cool, too. But on this particular day, those red eyes would again occupy your orbitals. You had been drinking and it uncovered some of the truths you hid deep within. "Son, I will always be your father, and no one can ever take that away from us. Things may not have been perfect between us, and I didn't have the money to buy you everything you wanted, but you will always be my son. I will never leave your side, even when you make mistakes," you pleaded as the tears rolled down. "I'm human. I made mistakes, but just know I'm trying, man. I am trying. I love you, son, more than you can ever know," you continued with a deep sadness in your voice. This happened to be around the time that mom married Curtis, and I believe you took his new responsibilities of taking care of our household and me as displaced love for you. But, Dad, no one could ever replace you. There was never a battleground for competition. I valued you both very differently. Dad, there was no comparison. You are my father. No matter what brick walls our relationship hits, you are my father.

Dad, I totally took that conversation for granted—blatantly disregarding your cry for validation. At the time, I was no older than 13 and completely oblivious to anything besides sports, school, and girls—in that order. I wasn't able to tap into my feelings at the time, let alone be able to articulate them to you or recognize when you required an ear to voice yours. Now that I'm older and mature enough to understand how imperative it is to demonstrate emotional intelligence, I failed you. Age is not a determining factor of maturity. I repeat—age is not a determining factor of maturity. And, Dad, I proved just how immature I was. I didn't even attempt to ask what was the cause of your deteriorating stableness or why you were crying. The only other time I saw you sob like that was when Papa passed. And to be honest, it made me uncomfortable. Yet in each case, I failed you. I didn't know what to say then at the funeral nor did I in the back of Granny's yard. I just assumed it was the liquor talking, and you were overly emotional because you were drunk.

It was moments like these that we needed more of. Again, I took that conversation for granted. I allowed the opportunity for us to actually connect on a deeper level to pass us by. Our communication required strengthening, but difficult conversations needed to be had. In addition to tempers flaring, I'm sure sparks would have flied. But we desperately needed to just talk, man. Dad, it was essential that you and I expressed ourselves, revealing all. From you, I required the Why.

Why did you drink, even after Papa died?
Why wasn't I, your son, enough to put the bottle down?
Why am I so stubborn? Are you?
Why do I have a short attention span when it comes to women? Do you?
Why did you ever feel as if I didn't love you?
Why do I have issues with allowing people in? Do you?
Why do we avoid discussing the real problems and act as if we

are okay?
Why am I so cold when it comes to my care of people? Are you?
Why did you think it was about buying me things versus spending time with me?
Why do I cry in the dark when no one is around? Do you?
Why didn't you hang around people your own age?
Why did you move to Callahan and let Grandma Elaine raise you?
Why am I afraid of asking for help? Are you?
Why didn't you just confide in me when you felt like life was winning?
Why do I feel powerless when unforeseen outcomes arise? Do you?
Why do we push people away when we're going through hard circumstances?
Why do I destroy every meaningful relationship I've ever had? Do you?
Why am I afraid of losing you and, in turn, losing myself? Are you?
Why can't we acknowledge that a father needs a son just as much as a son needs a father?

Dad, I realize we don't know each other. By allowing so much time to surpass us, we've grown into virtual strangers. As your seed, I'm sure there are undeniable similarities in our mannerisms, actions, speech, and of course our looks. "Ish, boy, you look just like your daddy," a common phrase I heard from every person who knew the both of us. I highly disagreed with them all. This may have stemmed from my indifference for you or drunken blindness of anger. No matter the reasoning, there was no escaping the truth. But where we differed, I would imagine, was in our approach and perspective on life. Having experienced and observed a variety of lifestyles from corporate America to the streets of the city, your teachings seemed irrelevant to the life I was pursuing.

I wanted you to educate me on the different facets of being a king. Society demonstrated time after time in a multitude of ways just how crowns weren't made to fit our heads as black males. Dad, society needed you to be there, especially well before its worst nightmare manifested into a violent reality. Just another lost nigga bound to be a domestic terrorist to his neighborhood, a menace to societal standards. Yeah, Dad, just another nigga. That's how I felt I was viewed—with all odds against me. The statistics weren't in my favor. You see, Dad, under these circumstances of not having you as a present guardian, society told me I had a 67% chance of being a high school dropout to a resident of a prison cell. I didn't stand a chance without guidance—the type of guidance Mom couldn't describe or offer, no matter how strong she proved to be. This was a rite of passage only you could gift me.

Dad, I needed you to tell me I was a man. As an African American male, I had no rites of passage into manhood. As described by Jawanza Kunjufu in his thought-provoking book *Countering the Conspiracy to Destroy Black Boys*:

> The ultimate goal of Rites of Passage is to prepare the boys for manhood. Our boys do not know when they're men, and it is the responsibility of men to teach them. If men do not fulfill this responsibility, boys will continue to define it from a physical perspective, e.g., making a baby, fights and the consumption of drugs, alcohol, clothes and cars.[1]

Dad, without your validation, I had no real understanding of where I was on my quest towards manhood. Lost in uncertainty, I didn't know the significance of what being a man was. What is a man? Am I a man? I constantly questioned. I couldn't even tell you what was required of a man a year before writing this book. I grew up well into my adulthood so misinformed on the makings of a man. It is sad. I fell under the impression that a man was the toughest one on the corner or the guy with the money to change his loved ones' lives. But I was unbelievably wrong. Dad, my narrowed mindedness created for me a map leading me nowhere but down roads of self-doubt, self-pity, and self-infliction of more grief. Constantly, I ignored the signs God laid out, showing me the better way—his way. Ignoring his blessings, employing my short-term memory, quickly forgetting how He delivered me from death and other times of agony.

Dad, the definition of a man didn't become vividly clear until I surrendered my unproven, no destination having ways. I had to take a leap of faith and trust God. Something I feared because that meant forfeiting control. This was the first step towards understanding my path and obtaining the answers to my questions. In our society, the American Dream is reiterated and guaranteed to those who exemplify a survivor's complex of hard work, ambition, and fierce determination. The American Dream is obtainable by those who have that dog in them, willing to take what's owed them versus accepting what people think they deserve. American Dreamers are people who get it done, the ski mask way, figuratively speaking, by all means. However, the truth is you can possess all of these impressive abilities, but still fall short of the accomplishments or person you long to achieve or to be. You see, what I learned the hard way, as someone who has a survivor's complex, is that relying on self can only get you so far. One still needs faith in God. That control must be given to Him, believing that he'll lead you beyond the figments of your imagination as the head of your life.

The devil had been trying to kill me from the very beginning. I was fighting a spiritual battle in the flesh without the armor of God—the only protection durable enough to see me through. I was bound to fail. I was unaware of the psychology of a man, having the ability to control my emotions, knowing when to exercise which. Dad, I needed more of your time to review and complete the curriculum of my *rite of passage*. You were the gatekeeper, possessing the instructions of spirituality, self-accountability, and service to my community.

I needed you to show me the importance of keeping God as the guide of my life and provider in times of struggle. It was vital that I learned from you, Dad, how to use the Bible as a living blueprint of life. Teaching me that perfection was unattainable but consistently self-improving was the goal. Dad, I needed you to lead me to the Book of Proverbs in which I could learn that fearing God would lead me to knowledge and wisdom as told in chapter one verse seven. This acknowledgment early in life could have saved me the stress of thinking I was in control of situations. Dad, I needed you to show me how to pray with power. Openly professing my faults, troubles, and simply building rapport with God. Praying on my knees in humility, giving all my troubles up to God. Dad, I wanted you to teach me.

Dad, being able to take responsibility for one's actions is testament to where a person is in life. Immaturity causes you to point the finger outward when fault rests inward. I lacked self-accountability. I wasn't honest with myself because of the damage inflicted in our relationship and the under-appreciation of my mother. The two of you deserved way more effort on my behalf. You brought me life; how could I dare to bring you strife? I disrespected you both on several occasions. Mom provided me with the necessities, but I had the nerve to have an attitude when she didn't buy me certain Jordan's. I was wrong, man, just wrong.

Reinforcement and correction from you could have reflected my wrongs in this and many other cases because a man openly acknowledges his mistakes.

Dad, I wanted you to teach me to be selfless. Men were created to be the head of households, entrusting that we know how to guide and demonstrate humanitarian-like qualities. In order to be the teacher, one must become an effective leader. It's vital you know how to listen to and put the wants and needs of others before your own desires. Demonstrating selflessness begins in the heart. Training your heart to tame the innate self-preservation monster in you takes a level of maturity only achievable through compassion. Having compassion for family members, friends or whomever around you births a feeling of joy, knowing you can ease their pain. Each time you're able to do this successfully without thinking of the inconvenience, it becomes easier. It's just like practicing the sport you are infatuated with becoming the greatest in. Take the same approach in practicing unselfish acts, giving yourself the experience to improve the makings of who you are on your path to manhood.

Dad, I rejected the idea of community and carried with me a full can of gas with matches to incinerate all bridges. You, of all people, knew the significance of cultivating relationships. You even tried to impress upon me the lesson, but I let it go in one ear and out the other. You really tried here and I can, without a doubt, say this one falls on me. "Community" is defined as *a social group of any size whose members reside in a specific locality, share government, and often have a common cultural and historical heritage*, according to diction-ary.com. The biggest takeaway here is the common aspects of culture and heritage in which members contribute to the continued growth of the community. Being active in the community adds to the devel-opment of all. Without the understanding that I needed people or any form of community, I was conspiring against myself.

From a man's perspective, I needed to learn how to empower a woman. You see, women are the givers of life, blessed with a womb to deliver miracles in birth. With that type of power, as described by Minister Louis Farrakhan, it's an abomination to disrespect a woman. I needed to know in what ways I could provide security for my significant other. That type of security that eased her mind, knowing I would solve any and all pressing issues we faced collec-tively—whether those issues were financial ones or required me liv-ing out faith over fear. Dad, I required the knowledge of knowing when to serve as a listener and not a solver all the time. I learned that, sometimes, being assertive with solutions to problems that are not mine is not always the sure answer.

I wanted you to teach me the importance of understanding when to pick my battles and when to simply say, "I'm sorry." Dad, learning to love a woman is a difficult art form, demanding patience, prayer, and perseverance. Love is work and the unspoken language of the world. And lastly, Dad, I needed you to demonstrate to me how to combat heartbreak or *The Fear in the Heart of A Man, Dedicated 2 My Heart,* as written by Tupac in his book of poems titled *The Rose That Grew From the Concrete*; in which he describes the firmness of a man's heart in all areas except love, for he demonstrates a unique vulnerability only revealed by heartbreak. Tupac meticulously crafts this poem as a warning to all men that love knows no limits and heartbreak knows no strangers.

This was one of the most necessary evils of life in heartbreak. It really teaches you what you are made of. The wide range of emotions and uncertainties—that pain has the power to mold your outlook on life. Dad, I wanted to hear your experiences with heartbreak—from what went wrong to what faults you assumed to how you moved on with your life.

Dad, I wanted to learn about generating and retaining wealth: 401 K's, IRA's, and building home equity. But instead, you taught me not to have any codefendants—do my dirt alone so no one can ever finger me in a courtroom. Not to say I was destined to be a criminal, but literally to watch whom I associated with and what I told them I did. A lesson I understood completely, but not one adding much value to my maturation into adulthood. But did I ever, even once, say, "Hey, Dad, I want to learn about x, y, and z."? No, I didn't. I just became furious and blamed you for my ignorance. So Dad, I failed you yet again. I failed in my communication to ask for what I wanted. You have not because you asked not, and I'll be damned it wasn't true because I never asked you for any of it.

Dad, what else can I say except I'm sorry? Sorry for my abandonment of you, leaving you without a son to raise far beyond the years of his youth. Learning is a continuous practice of acquiring knowledge with the desire to grow wiser. I attempted to do it without you, a clear mistake. I'm sorry not only for the hurtful things I said to you like, "I don't care if we speak again," or "I'll be a way better man than you ever will," but also for my unsolicited actions. I never thought about the harm of such condescending words damaging you. For years, you were my punching bag. Each blame equating to a right or left hook to the midsection of the heavy bag while each mistake I made—so easily avoidable through your teaching—turned into jabs. The haymakers and power blows were the result of me acknowledging I needed you. These blows hurt us both. Throwing such a high volume of haymakers—it sucked the energy out of me, leaving me breathless.

Dad, I remember getting the phone call you had been rushed to the hospital for emergency surgery. The thought of losing you quickly erased any malice I held in my heart. That defining moment of truth revealed the power of love. Never did I want to see you suffer, or even worse, die—especially before the two of us were able to create peace and truly reap the benefits of our bond. Love had shown itself in its purest form—honesty. I was able to come to ill-advised terms with not speaking with you, but I knew forgiving myself wasn't a possibility if you died.

And just like that, Dad, you were gone. That night in surgery you died, twice. I was nowhere to be found, didn't even drive home when I got the news you were resuscitated. I got the call from your girlfriend as she sat in the waiting room, waiting for updates from your surgeon. Her voice faint with fear, her vocal inflections fluctuated with every syllable, but her message was clear. "Ish, I don't know if your dad is going to make it." I sat there in silence, attempting to wrap my mind around the thought of losing you.

Huh?
What does she mean she doesn't know if you're going to make it?
Are the doctors missing something?

I just don't understand what is going on.
What was the last thing I said to you?
How could I be so stupid?

Dad, I was ashamed of myself. I allowed years of stubbornness to keep me away. You needed me. I was no doctor or miracle worker, but my presence and support could have lifted you up. If anything, I could have lifted up the family, especially Granny. No mother imagines having to bury her child, the one she gave life to, watching her own creation become its own. I hung up the phone, still sitting on the couch. Not once did it occur to me that I should have rushed from Orlando to Jacksonville.

I was scared I would lose you. I was scared you'd be mad at me for treating you so foul. In the end, I was too scared to swallow my pride to come be by your side, possibly having to say goodbye. I thought back to when Papa died and never getting to say goodbye to him either. It was evident the lesson wasn't learned to value family or life.

Results came back. They revealed diverticulitis. You were diagnosed with this extremely painful condition of the intestines in which small pouches form on the colon with bacteria causing severe inflammation. Your condition had gotten so bad that your small intestine exploded, filling your body with dangerous waste, getting into your bloodstream. We hadn't spoke in months. Just another break in communication. These were routine. This time I stopped talking to you because you cursed me out for not letting you know I made it safely to Atlanta in June. The whole time I held animosity towards you because you didn't send me the money you had promised. Money I didn't even ask you for. I had the audacity not to talk to you over $25. Dad, saying I'm sorry is almost meaningless because so many mistakes were made on my part. I was so close to losing you over $25. How could I ever make that up to you? For that measly amount of money, I could get gas, maybe a meal, but it wasn't enough to buy your life back. It wasn't enough to cover funeral services. It wasn't enough to pay for a tombstone saying, "A loving father rests here." A measly $25.

That's really it, huh? You let $25 be the reason you would never speak to your father again.
And still you walk around mad at him?
You worthless scumbag.
You got the nerve to show face and appear sad?
Every time you even think about missing him, just think about that $25 he owes you, punk.

I have yet to forgive myself for this.

After taking a few days to come to my senses, I drove from Orlando straight to Orange Park hospital. I was so nervous because I didn't know where we stood or even if you wanted to see me. I felt uncomfortable being around you because it didn't feel genuine. There was so much between us unresolved that I felt phony just sweeping it under the rug, which we both continued to stumble on continuously. It was becoming exhausting for the both of us. It was apparent we both wanted to move past the on and off relationship we had. You lying in that hospital bed in overbearing pain, watching my grandmother sob, the rest of the family quiet—it reminded me of the scene of Papa in the hospital.

It was unreal how parallel the situations were. Even as a kid, I still remember the roles everyone portrayed. Uncle Aaron wasn't one to enjoy hospitals. He couldn't even do it for the loved one in bed suffering. He did everything he could to avoid spending any considerable amount of time inside the halls of any medical facility. Auntie sat there watching with a concerned look all across her face. Grandmother, again, just sobbing. This now was the exact setup as when Papa died. Dad, I felt just like Uncle Aaron. I couldn't take it either. I imagined we shared the same thoughts of losing you—his older brother, my father—but we never to this day have spoken about our feelings in either instance. I didn't know what to say to anyone in the room, no one had seen me in months because I rarely came to visit. I rarely called. Just a family member who was easier to love years ago as a child. But now I was just a distant relative who didn't appreciate the blessing of having a family. I took everyone for granted.

    Before I left, you asked me to stay behind to talk. And I'll never forget your words, "Son, no matter what we got going on, man, I still love you. You're my seed, all that other bullsh*t don't matter." I hugged you, still with no words and left. I always thought what if that was our last time seeing each other, and how I just left without expressing to you how much I appreciated you for any of what you'd done for me or anything. I had to live with my mistreatments of you without regret. I felt justified in my actions because you had always managed to find a way to get under my skin to force me to distance myself from you.

    One thing, I noticed after you got out of the hospital after spending 27 straight days in there, you came out a new person. You were full of life. This was something I had never seen in you before. You began to take the initiative to restore our relationship. It was amazing to see the change in our conversations shift from the sports desk at ESPN or the interworkings of women to God's purpose over our lives and living in the image of His only begotten son Jesus. I was accustomed to always having these types of faith-filled conversations with my mother, but experiences with the afterlife brought you closer to our Savior. It was astonishing to watch your transition and your willingness to admit your faults as a man. I never saw you display such vulnerability—while sober that is. Hearing you talk with such a renewed mind was refreshing.

    Through this rebuilding process, you taught me one of the most important lessons about people to date: people won't change until they are ready. One cannot force people to just give up the habits of their being; it's a part of who they are and what they have known during the course of their life. Every person has his own day of reckoning in which he realizes he can't go any longer with his current way of living. Dad, for years I wanted you to stop drinking, but I was oblivious to the stage of life you were in. I couldn't press fast forward on your self-discovery. You taught me that when a man or woman is ready to implement changes in their life he or she will, independent of the opinions or pressure of individuals around them.

But Dad, that wasn't the only time I've yet to let go. Back in 2013, when I was working for Statewide during my senior year in college, you couldn't work and asked me for some money because you needed it. Not once ever had you previously asked me for money or anything else for that matter. I reassured you that I'd see what I could do. However, I never called you back. I didn't even check my finances to see what I could spare. You always taught me to believe a person's actions and not their words. As we concluded that conversation, I hung up the phone and said, "I love you." But my actions demonstrated otherwise. I showed you just how much I didn't care about what you were going through, putting my own personal needs before yours. How could I deny you help when I was blessed enough to work? I didn't have excess money to give away, but that wasn't the point. For family, you learn to make sacrifices and figure out challenging situations, not run from them just as I did. When it came down to choosing between you or myself, you always came second.

Naturally, by ignoring you and your request, you responded in emotional outrage. You called me cursing and yelling at me until I hung up not wanting to hear any of what you had to say. I felt disrespected by you taking that tone and using vulgarity with me. You knew that was one thing I never stood to endure from you or anyone else. I always shut down, cutting off the offending individual instantly. Dad, I admit you had every right to express your frustrations with my selfishness. I failed you as a son. I had to sit and think about how Papa would also be disgusted with me treating you like this or the day that I would have a son turn his back on me in my time of need. The universe would pay me back for how I treated you, one way or another.

Dad, writing this chapter from the heart shows me just how much you've taught me since my days as a child. I played back certain memories with and without you, but I was still able to identify the influence you've had over a huge portion of my decisions. Even if the choice was made out of spite, so I wouldn't be the second coming of you, Lil Larry, you helped mold me into the man I am today. The man you've always been proud of, for so long and regardless of all the grief I've caused you. You taught me that people make mistakes. It's inevitable and loving someone supersedes those blunders. "Son, I'm going to be there for you whether you become the President or America's most wanted. I'll never leave your side," you reinforced this message to me for years. And Dad, you kept your word through it all. That type of dedication and patience is admirable. You demonstrated valiant perseverance. You've accepted my imperfections and the time has come for me to accept yours just the same while acknowledging my faults as well.

Together we're capable of helping each other. You're able to give me the wisdom of your years of experience, and I'm able to show you the result of your teachings—avoiding the obstacles you fell to. I can also show you my abilities in creating my own story, taking a path much different than yours. A path without the drinking, the drugs, or other vices. A better path that a father can only want for his son, surpassing your output with your blessing and guidance. Dad, together I want to strengthen the Brown family name, but only if we do it together.

I remember the time when I was ashamed to bear the same last name as you. I told my mom I wanted to change my name, and as a mother, she was conflicted. She wanted to support me in everything I did—in reason, of course—but a last name change would be something that came with huge ramifications. I was only 16 when I was ready to re-create who I was and step into a new identity, one that erased me from your shadow. Ismael Rashid Williamson, the bitter, spiteful teenager who thought he knew it all, wanting nothing but to hurt you, Dad. "Son, you need to let anger towards your father go. It's holding you back from the blessings God has for you," mom would warn me.

Dad, you picked an amazing woman to have your seed because she was always a huge supporter of us having a relationship. "Boop, have you talked to your Dad," she asked frequently. She also pleaded with me to go see you. "Son, you should go see your Dad to see how he's doing. I'm sure he would like that." I know things between you two did not work out in your relationship, but I admired the respect the both of you had for each other. Both of you always shared praise for the roles each played in my life. Dad, you would tell me all the time how much you appreciated my mom for raising me the right way. I knew deep down you felt as if she did it alone. To be honest, growing up, I couldn't have agreed with you more. But now, Dad, I can introduce the facts and confidently say we were both wrong. Dad, your role in my life, although unconventional, was dependable. In every instance when I needed you, you were there. The things about life that mom couldn't teach me, you taught me.

You reinforced Papa's lesson of living with no regrets and standing firm on the solid foundation of every decision I made. This taught me to meticulously ponder on the small details before making choices. I would over analyze everything before confidently deciding on anything. This lesson challenged my mind to think holistically, ignoring nothing. I appreciated this lesson because it showed me to never look back or rethink decisions as if they were mistakes, but rather to navigate the consequences of each action with a smile on my face. The duality of so much thinking comes in the form of over doing it. Second-guessing myself is not what you intended. Overthinking stressed me out all too often. When I walked you through some of my thoughts, you laughed when I said I didn't know why. You responded with, "You don't trust yourself, so you overcompensate by thinking of all outcomes, hoping to avoid error. Son, you have to be comfortable with who you are. Your choices will shape your life, but they won't cement it. Make a choice and move forward, learn from everything."

That conversation taught me there was no such thing as a mistake as long as I considered all outcomes. Each decision, in turn, would prove to be a learning lesson, sharpening my skills as I grew older. Mistakes were not a waste of time, but a misuse of my time. I capitalized on all opportunities thanks to this lesson. I was able to connect with two generations of Brown men and am able now to pass on some wisdom to a fourth upon the birth of my seed one day.

Dad, I hope you can find forgiveness in your heart for all the times I failed you. I am ready to be your son and move past all of the wrongs of our yesterdays. I love you and appreciate you more than I've ever let you know until now. I pray this book reaches you and that you understand why I chose this medium as a communication channel. My thought process is this may be the only way to avoid any interruption in what I had to say, and I was able to unleash everything. I did not do this to cause further damage or to hurt you. I want to show you that I am able to accept ownership for my mistreatment and bitterness towards you for the past 15-plus years. Dad, I am free of it all. I want us to walk hand-in-hand in grace, learning each other, figuring out life together. I know for years you thought I never listened to you. I heard it all, but I had to go out into the world, bump my head a few times and scrape my knees until I realized you were right.

So I ask that you please forgive me, father.

Your son,

Fish D

A WOMANIZER

THE ENEMY: *Don't trust a woman, the Bible tells you that! Get yours and keep it moving. Love will get you killed, leave you broke or contemplating life.*

I CHEATED ON EVERY GIRLFRIEND OR WOMAN I EVER CARED ABOUT. Why? Because I didn't have any respect for a woman's worth. I hid behind the false pretense of *I'm a good guy.* It was just so easy for me. I had a gift of gab for obtaining a woman's mind. If she gave me her time, I'd pillage her heart. It came as a game to me. Women were chess pieces. I'd carefully plan my next three moves based on her receptiveness to my game.

I was a misogynistic womanizer. To describe a womanizer, it was someone who rode the high horse of taking advantage of the tenderness of women, constantly abusing their trust, their hearts, and their futures. As a womanizer, I inflicted uncapped damage on all the women who ever considered loving such a self-centered monster who prided himself on maintaining a rotation simultaneously. The perception of having multiple women at my disposal is what I praised.

I thought it made me a man—being able to hold power over women the way I watched all the men around me do. From my father to my homeboys to the celebrities I adored. They all showed me how to dishonor women, calling them out of their names, referencing them to female dogs, garden tools, and other degrading terms. I learned to use them for personal gain, demonstrating no loyalty, simply pilfering their genuineness.

These teachings gave me the blueprint for how to cement my impact on each of them long term, forcing them to run away, run far away from anything reminding them of the hell I'd put them through. Whether it was the way they were approached, talked to, or treated, they would have to combat their fears of meeting another womanizer. I admitted to being a man, but only had the output of a boy who valued the opinions of other lost pupils. Being a womanizer was glorified in my community, throughout the music we created and to which we danced the night away.

This one for my bitches, This one for hoes; but never one for my Nubian Queens or beautiful black women—every single song I listened to addressed women by these derogative terms. My favorite artists of my primitive years included the likes of Snoop Dogg, DMX, The Hot Boys or The Diplomats instilled in me the value of exploiting women for everything I could take from them. Bar by bar they glamorized the exchange of power through sexual intercourse; leaving the woman with nothing once she exposed her treasures, only to be shamed for her promiscuous ways. This music that I nodded my head to, sung word for word and gained genuine joy from once the beat dropped was conditioning me to destroy the confidence and security of women. And sure enough, I followed suit calling woman hoes in causal conversation stealing their essence.

I believed women were expendable. They were like the seasons: they came and they went. But you knew they would always come back, never lasting forever. So there was no need to panic or fret over one. It'll only be temporary and with the ratio of women to men in this world, I would be just fine. I was brainwashed and didn't realize it until I started to see all the women I hurt move on happily ever after—without me. They found real men. Men who respected their value, healed their pain, completed their incompleteness, and wiped their tears instead of creating them—and best friends in love. They found exactly what I wasn't.

The worst part was I knew better. I had observed my mother go through bad relationships. She taught me to be a gentleman—from opening car doors to standing next to the street when walking down sidewalks. My mother showed me how to be chivalrous. She also told me women paid close attention to the way a man treats other women in his life, such as his mother, sisters, and aunts. They viewed it as a precursor to how a man would treat them if loved. Well mom, I can honesty say this wasn't necessarily true. I had close relationships with my mother and sister, whom I adored. So how could I do those things to other women? The lies I would concoct, the people I would drag down in my elaborate stories, and the trail of tears I left behind. A trail that I myself ended up traveling on as well. Pain is subjective, leaving it within the mind to create obstacles, preventing a speedy recovery. Through these encounters, I was hurt by something greater I had failed to acknowledge. I was a hub of pain, wrapped in a smile and impressive conversation. It was simple: my mother couldn't show me how to empower or love a woman; only a man could show me how to honor a Queen.

While in college, I learned a lot about myself through my relationships with women. Some of them helped shape me into a better man while others were vessels of sinful pleasure. Regardless of how I segmented them, I was able to see where I went wrong in every case and how unbeneficial they were because of my selfishness. Through this chapter, I want to detail two relationships specifically that had lasting effects on me moving forward and growing up in general. The lessons learned from these women are priceless, and if I could say one last thing to them it would be:

Sorry for the man you met, the lack of ownership I took in our demise, and the pain I inflicted that you had to carry into future relationships. You didn't deserve that. I did not uphold the original representation of self that I introduced you to. May you continue to shine and develop with the love in your hearts that once attracted me.

SADE – THE "SOLDIER OF LOVE"

"Your problem is you don't care about anybody but yourself. You only talk when its convenient for you and at the expense of those who really love and care about you. Ismael, you're so damn selfish!"

Sade, Sade…where do I start? She was the most determined, strong willed person I've ever met. When this girl wanted something, you couldn't find the balls to tell her no. Sade would convince you that the answer she wanted was the exact same you intended to give to her. Her gift and curse lied in her ability to love. Her love was fierce; it came with an abundance of passion and pain. There was no measure to her love. And through our time together, I discovered the root of her passion—a reoccurring cycle of people abandoning her. This was something we shared, and she reflected my deeper abandonment issues. Our struggles and personal drive connected us to each other like magnets. We often broke bread feasting with chips on our shoulders.

Sade was a survivalist and that was something I comprehended. Growing up, that's what her life consisted of—not enjoying a childhood but surviving without her biological parents. She reminded me a lot of my mother, both being champions of life and finding ways to win the toughest battles life threw at them. The commonalities between the two of them were scary.

They both relied on their independence over all because of the troublesome circumstances they were raised in. My mother grew in the Magnolia Projects located off 1st street in Elizabeth, New Jersey, before moving to a drug-induced neighborhood on the north side of Jacksonville, Florida, at the age of 11. She grew up in a single-parent home headed by my grandmother who had a 7th grade education only and who demanded she fight for everything she had to raise her three children. Courtney, also known as CoCo by her children and close friends, was my grandmother's name. She pushed her kids to be better than she and to pursue graduating from high school. Unfortunately, she was only able to witness her two oldest children graduate from high school due to her untimely death to colon cancer.

My mother was only 18 years old when her CoCo passed. She was still a child herself with the whole world to take on alone with no guidance or further instruction from the one who brought her here. Sade also knew what it was like to lose a parent at a relatively young age. And much like my mother, Sade had to rely on instincts of survival to teach herself the lessons of life her father wasn't able to share in the natural world. The fight in them both grew over time, giving them unlimited fuel to constantly defy odds, prove people wrong, and achieve goals they set for themselves. Their fight was born of death. There was no innate fear; therefore, it gave them an undeniable edge in taking on unchartered waters. Nothing was comparable to the strife they had already endured, so everything else proved to be an appetizer, barely satisfying their hunger for fulfillment.

Another quality they shared that was less desirable was the ease of cutting people off, ending relationships across multiple dynamics, ranging from lovers to family members and friends. Each had difficult times fighting for relationships. Once people crossed them or did things they disagreed with, they washed their hands of them. People had expiration dates and the desire to hold on to spoiled relationships wasn't a priority. This too was something I was an expert at.

My mom would warn me not to be so easily defeated in my dealings with people and encouraged me to preserve relationships. She would shake her head in laugher when I told her how I'd stopped dealing with certain people and excommunicated them from my life. "Son, you can't do that. I'm telling you this from my own personal interactions that I wish I could have given more effort. You have to learn to accept people for who they are. In time, everyone will show his or her true colors. You just have to believe them and stop expecting people to act or think like you. I was the same way," she advised me. I didn't see the need to deal with people's inconsistencies. It beyond frustrated me.

Sade and I were too much alike in ways that weren't beneficial to either of us. Our personalities were both type A, not willing to bow down to anyone. We argued a lot, way more than we should have. Compromising wasn't in my arsenal of skills. I was right 100 percent of the time, not leaving her with much to claim as victories. And when she combated, I shut her out, giving her one-word responses if any at all. It was completely disrespectful on my behalf. I apologized only when it was convenient for me, which consisted of me growing exhausted with her raised voice, wanting her company, or completely done with the complaining. If a situation wasn't benefiting me, there was no apology.

With Sade, I wasn't honest. I was immature and a manipulative person. She was older, more put together than any other woman I pursued—and a challenge. After she let her guard down, showing willingness to give me a chance, I made her pay for her vulnerability. I rewarded her with half-heartedness, lies, and false commitments. I wasn't ready for the type of relationship she wanted, but at the time I thought that being brutally honest would hurt her. I demonstrated full incompetence in maturity by putting forth false truths, by leading her on to believe we wanted the same things. From time to time, I would demonstrate some of the characteristics she desired from a man: an ambitious leader providing guidance for his better half through transparency and romantic reciprocation. I cared deeply for Sade, and for that reason, I wanted to give her all I had but refused the both of us that privilege.

I was unsuccessful in telling Sade I was not really ready for exclusivity because my mindset at the time valued quantity of women over the pricelessness of one I could connect with. In my failure, I continued to pursue other women behind her back, searching for validation of my peers that I got women, and there was no doubt about it. This shined a light on deeper issues I had. This was what I saw the men around me do when I was growing up—whether it was my father, cousins, or uncle. They all had a collection of women to choose from. They all were womanizers. It appeared to me like a hobby or game of sorts. I assumed that's what I was supposed to do as a man.

I was carrying baggage from a previous relationship that I needed to learn from and then let go. I was allowing the past to cloud my judgment all while selling dreams at discounted rates. Beautiful elaborate dreams full of promise and unadulterated hope I sold to women, including Sade, casting me as the perfect gentleman. The guy every girl desired to take home to her parents, the one who opened doors, brought flowers, and exhibited the basics of a good man. Those were things in me, but I tiptoed between what was in me and what was around me. I found myself too afraid to open up in dating. The thought of being gravely affected or damaged by another woman was enough to deny the next an opportunity to show me otherwise. It truly wasn't fair but a testament that time does not heal all, merely a component of healing. When only employing time to heal, you're operating at a disadvantage, allowing the mind to take you through phases.

Phase one is the *blaming game,* in which your mind searches for someone to apply the condemnation upon that ultimately falls on self at the end of it. Blaming others can only last for so long because the finger-pointing or constant murderous thoughts do not affect those you're blaming—only you. After coming to that understanding and witnessing them happily post the relationship, you move into Phase two: *fabricated happiness.* In this stage, you begin to become adventurous, attempting to find solace in things or people, allowing you to mentally run away from the issue. You're creating distractions for yourself and further pushing the real problem to the side, which continues to obstruct your path to full healing. Internally, you begin to question yourself:

> *What am I doing? Is this really me?*
> *Does this really make me happy?*
> *Am I losing myself?*

In this stage, you also realize just how sick you are without that person because the one thing you've been sure of your whole life you now doubt more than ever. From here, move into Phase three: *even tomorrow is yesterday.* In by far the most difficult stage, the realization hits in later relationships, regardless of how much time has elapsed, that subconsciously everything from that one relationship is still having a significant impact. You have built what seems like the Berlin Wall around your heart, preventing any new experiences in, ones that mend the brokenness inside. Everyone you deal with is punished, paying for someone else's sins. Is it fair? No, not at all. But it is a reflective moment that proves you haven't fully healed. And ladies and gentleman, I have been through the three phases repetitively. I was on a hamster wheel, relying on time to heal me, punishing Sade continuously. She was my canvas painting—the red strokes of pain in her eyes, blue strokes of tears falling from them, and black smears from her makeup.

With Sade, I could tell my most intimate moments as well as my dreams, free from judgment with ease. The atmosphere was always welcoming for burdensome conversation, and she not only actively listened, she provided logical feedback with directional advice. Older than I, she was able to eloquently express her wisdom on a variety of topics on which I had no knowledge. It promoted my growth and abilities on being conscious as to how I would navigate new arising problems. Knowing just how much she tried to alleviate any discomfort when communicating was also reflective of my inability to come forth with my reservations I had about dating. I was more of a coward than a man when the opportunities for me to come clean about my insecurities arose.

She witnessed a lot of my ups and downs during our time together. I was stressed out with more responsibilities than a plate to hold them. My past was creeping up on me, and she knew I wasn't going to talk to her about my issues. "Ish, you got to talk to somebody, dawg. Whatever you are holding is crushing you. It's becoming more prevalent every day," she said with concern. Knowing she couldn't help me gravely affected her. She was so accustomed to solving problems, so not being able to fix me was problematic. "You should go to therapy," she recommended.

"I'm not going to no shrink to tell my problems. Naw, that's whack and not going to happen," I quickly replied.

"I wish you would just try it. I know it doesn't seem cool or even manly. But it's helpful. Talking and releasing whatever it is will be therapeutic. I even know someone you can talk to on campus, Dr. Gilmore. She's helped sooooo many students. I'm telling you, she's off the chain," Sade said.

The thought of going to complain about life to anyone wasn't my cup of tea. My perception was archaic in the idea that I was supposed to figure out my own problems.

A therapist?
She a woman; how can she relate to anything I got going on?
It's weak to go sit and express my feelings.
I shouldn't even be feeling in the first place.
Sade don't know what she's talking about.
I can't be looking weak out here.

But after a few more failed tests in school because I was mentally distracted, I decided to give Dr. Gilmore a shot. I walked up to her office on the 2nd floor of the student union, and introduced myself. Before you knew it, I was spilling my life to a stranger. Sade was right. I had reached my breaking point. Any attempts to mask my issues by obtaining so many leadership roles or activities allowed me to run away from being surrounded by myself again.

Dr. Gilmore was a tremendous help in getting me to understand that I was holding on to things that occurred in my childhood. Well, my younger years because a childhood is not what I had. As a youth, I was thrown into the struggles of life too soon. There was no room for a child. Life hardened my heart, closing out the thrills of my youth. She explained the longer I avoid dealing with myself, the longer these issues would live on in me. She gave her unbiased thoughts on every situation I presented to her. We spoke about everything from my rocky relationship with Dad to my commitment issues with women. When I was wrong, she never held her tongue. When I thought I was crazy feeling like no one could relate, she provided assurance that my problems were not unique. Sade was responsible for creating this connection that began the process of my healing.

Sade specialized in acts of service as described by Gary Chapman in his best-selling book *The 5 Love Languages*. This love language was defined by one's ability to put love in action and making your love come to life. Acts of services were executed through listening to your significant other's wants, needs, and desires and demonstrating them through effort. Sade was always looking for new ways to prove to me she wasn't like any other woman I'd met before. For example, if she came over and saw clothes that needed folding or washing, she did it with no questions asked. Initially, I thought it was cool, and why not? Shoot, I was winning. What guy didn't want a chick to do his laundry? But after a while, I knew I wasn't reciprocating the same effort and it bothered me. And in typical Ismael fashion, I didn't stop her—just continued to abuse her love.

The more I got to know her, the more the pressure mounted on my shoulders to change my ways, but I never did. Sade required very little of me yet still showed me so much. I remember Sade sharing with me how she lost her father in a fatal car crash and how late-night driving evoked those same eerie feelings. When I would go back home to Jacksonville, I always left late after 7pm or even later in the midnight hours. It terrified the hell out of her that I did this, and she asked me several times to just wait until the morning or at least let her know when I made it safely. I couldn't even do that. All I thought about was myself. Giving her the assurance that I was alive and well was asking too much. It was disgusting to treat Sade or any woman this way and insensitive of me considering the root of her concern.

She didn't deserve a scumbag like me. She deserved better, a better I couldn't give her. I was too focused on myself and always willing to choose me over her. Years after we each moved on with our lives, I picked up the phone to dial her number and apologize, but I ended up convincing myself not to.

It's too late now.
Calling her will only stir up situations she's forgotten.
I'm not trying to get into a tongue war with her.
I deserve it, though.
She should curse me out, using every one she can think of.
Maybe one day I'll do it.

I owed her several apologies but had no courage to face her. Not even over the phone. No, I didn't still have feelings for her. But as an adult, I'd come to the point in life when it was time to right my wrongs. My lies had held me hostage long enough. She earned the peace of mind of closure—obtaining the answers to the thousands of questions she had. The answers in the form of keys unlocking the shackles of doubting herself in relationships because of my shortcomings and dishonesty. Sade taught me that a person's feelings are never wrong. She emphasized the value of being able to openly express the depths of what made her smile to what caused her to cringe or cry. Feelings are not always meant to be agreed upon but should always be considered and respected.

The relationship taught me what you inflict on others comes back—gunning you down in the street, a story for the news to polarize people on TV like blacks dying at the hands of white officers. I didn't want to hurt anyone anymore. I also learned from Sade that honesty is important in managing expectations. This holds true in allowing your words, "I'm not ready for anything serious," not to contradict your actions of constantly spending time with someone. My actions didn't match my words, creating a parasitic situation.

AALIYAH – THE "ONE IN A MILLION"

"But I don't see the end goal, and you opened my eyes to that. I've been holding on to something that doesn't have a concrete future."

"No end goal? What the hell do you mean? I've done nothing but…"

These were the words that would cause me to dive into a downward spiral.

Words that shattered my heart
Words that caused me to lose confidence in myself
Words that resulted in sleepless nights
Words that caused me to go days without eating
Words that helped me lose almost 40 lbs. in little more than 3 months
Words that forced me to second-guess myself, my decision of moving to DC

Words carrying pain only comparable to the death of my grandfather…

How was I supposed to go on? Her breaking up with me and not even a month into me moving in—it destroyed me and all my newfound happiness. I took 11 steps backwards. My thoughts became engulfed by the idea that she quit! Literally gave up on us.

All the sh*t we been through and she gone leave me. Just gone throw almost three years away. None of that meant anything to her? Was I not worth giving a chance? I know I messed up plenty in the past, but this was my opportunity to redeem myself. I even went as far as expressing my interest in wanting to ask for her hand in the union of marriage— the beautiful, unconventional journey of forever.

The separation felt deeper than losing a girlfriend. It was equivalent to losing grips with reality. She was the only thing my heart and mind ever agreed on. She made me better. Aaliyah was the living, breathing testament of God's careful crafting of any human being. She was the purest form of beauty that sprouted seeds of joy, internally blossoming into the apple of my eye externally. She managed to take power away from the things I felt insecure about in the midst of shameful doubt. "Let me lick your gap," she would say and, oh, how I cringed at the idea of anyone appreciating what I attempted to hide in conversation and pictures. "I can't wait to get this gap closed," I would tell her time and again. "Ish, when you smile, show your teeth. You have a great smile. There's nothing to hide. Your gap is a part of who you are and if you close it, I'm leaving you, " she would reply half jokingly. She was the only person to ever admire my gap throughout my entire life, and I truly didn't realize just how much that meant to me until I lost her. There could be no one else. My mind turned against me instantly as I began to blame myself for losing her.

> *She didn't quit; you just weren't man enough to stay in Orlando and fight it out. You left that girl when she inconvenienced herself for you. She extended her hard earned resources to feed you, and how do you pay her back, by leaving? Then you have the nerve to make her feel lousy for making the best decision for herself—the same way you did by taking the job in Virginia. Double standard, huh, Ismael? You were dead weight holding her down, and now she's able to move on with her life, free of you! Remember that time you cheated and told thousands of lies to cover it up? She should have left you.*

Empty,
Blank,
Barren,
Abandoned,
Vacant,
Deserted,

No one word could describe what I felt. Maybe a combination of them could explain a fraction of me. Nothing made sense about her decision in my eyes. I really thought it would last forever. I never doubted that.

A sickness fell over me, one that wasn't treatable by any procedures by the world's finest surgeons or curable by any doctor-prescribed medication. I'd contracted one of the most common illnesses known to man. Everyone who'd ever lived and loved managed to catch a case of *heartbreak*. The normalcy of such a devastating moment didn't ease the blow of the frustrations or the pain that ensued. Some people never recover, becoming bitter, growing with resentment in their heart, affecting every relationship thereafter. Phrases like *I'll never love again, Love is for suckas*, or *F*ck love* become reoccurring sayings in the healing process—a universal coping method to deflect. You see, with love, it's not like a light switch you can just turn off when that person pisses you off, does you wrong, or does what's truly best for her in that given moment. Love is more of a tattoo on your back that you know is there, even though you can't visually see it. Love's power is stronger than any other feeling, and finding it in a human form is borderline a miracle. But to have that love severed—unexpectedly—is purely devastating.

During my period of bereavement, I began to lose my appetite. Food couldn't fill me up. What I was hungry for was Aaliyah's love. No grocery store within a thousand miles sold this or could recommend something with similar taste. I desired her validation. She gave me confidence in every thing I did. Her approval gave me a sense of cool because, either way, she would support my decisions. Aaliyah empowered me in my areas of deficiencies as well as in my insecurities. Mentally, I couldn't control the frequency of the *Whys*.

Why did she not want me?
Why wasn't I good enough?
Why couldn't we still communicate afterwards? Did I really want that?
Why was she the only thing my mind was able to think about?
Why can't I just forget her?
Why did I let her obtain so much power over my emotions?
Why doesn't she seem affected by this at all?
Why weren't the memories of all the good times enough to fight for us?
Why didn't I open more car doors for her?

Why couldn't I take the initiative to plan more dates and activities for us to do?
Why wasn't I more open about our relationship on social media? Is that what she wanted?
Why couldn't anyone understand what I was going through?
Why was I not able to focus at work?
Why did I have to go run to the bathroom and cry in a stall numerous times?
Why was I so stupid?

The loss of appetite grew into sleep deprivation—not being able to escape the horrors of the night. I would lie in bed for hours just punishing myself on where I went wrong and attempting to uncover some type of solace in taking the blame. The pressure became too much and the frustration of not being able to turn off my thoughts caused me to self-medicate. It wasn't even two weeks later that I began popping Benadryl pills just to go to sleep. I feared my thoughts more than I did an overdose. The pills didn't work, so I stopped taking them with water but with Nyquil. I was so broken and confused. This was the only thing that made some type of sense. I desperately needed to sleep. After just starting a new job, I had to compartmentalize this as a home problem and not a work problem. But it was inevitable the two worlds would collide. Focusing at work became an oxymoron. I became so overwhelmed that I would find myself balling silently in the bathroom stalls, praying no one heard the sniffling.

Man, get yourself together. Forget her; she forgot you.
You moved all the way up here for this job and gone just blow it?
You think you sad now, imagine getting fired and being broke again with no money to pay bills?
That's real pain.
You gone be alright.

I had to go back into the office with a smile on my face and prove to them why hiring me was the perfect choice.

I had to talk to someone, anyone, about it and find some type of explanation as to why this happened. I found myself talking to anyone who wasn't deaf or willing to listen. This practice was an unwarranted attempt at obtaining answers from people who couldn't, I repeat couldn't, provide me with any of the answers I needed. Only Aaliyah could. But as a drunkard of unforgiveness and pride, I allowed my intoxication to cloud my judgment. I was still angry at the sorrow she inflicted. I felt her decision was selfish and did not incorporate my feelings whatsoever. The pride spilled out from my eyes as tears and through my nose as mucus. I was convinced she needed to reach out to me to talk since she decided to part ways. If I did so, it was a sign of weakness, being at her mercy.

Then again, I didn't know if I was going to be able to handle her answers; my emotional control wasn't that great. So I figured it was better if I didn't reach out to her. Was this a wise choice or a mistake? Looking back it was a combination of both. Wise that I understood that emotionally I wasn't mature enough to communicate my feelings in a conversation that omitted anger or an argumentative spirit. It was wise of me to hold off before causing more damage in our already disenfranchised relationship. Yes, I still loved her and regardless of what we'd been through, I still valued her heart. I couldn't live with hurting her further than I'd already done.

In contrast, it was a mistake not to seek proper closure. By leaving that door open, the unknowns would continuously linger in my thoughts—whether in the front or back of my mind. I'd always think about the *Whys* and *What Ifs*. A self-imposed mistake can stain your confidence in making the best decisions moving forward. You begin second-guessing everything, which can prove unhealthy, making you indecisive. And in relationships, demonstrating indecisiveness is a key indicator one is not ready to be fully vested in the success of companionship. More so as a man, I've learned you are looked to for guidance and per the Bible, you are the head.

My mother taught me a lesson in love: one plus one equals one. It wasn't until this relationship that I understood that lesson. The hardest equation of life is making that equation work. Bringing two very different people together and forming one single union. Finding someone who understood you, accepting your flaws to love you all the same—it was a blessing. I will go as far to say it's border-line a miracle finding your soul mate.

Others bounce back without a second thought about their former partner. Heartbreak wasn't a unique problem people experienced.

Just two weeks prior to this calamity, we had a conversation to discuss our options and the chances of living in the same city sooner than later. I tiptoed around this conversation because I couldn't be forceful or leading. It would have been selfish of me to just demand anything of her, especially in regards to moving so far from the things she loved—her family, her career, her whole life.

Carefully, I replayed how this conversation would go in my head, from possible responses she could give or questions she might have. I had major selling points that applied to the things she cared greatly about. Career being at the top of that list. I conducted research on the job market in the District and surrounding areas. She was in the workforce two years already as an assistant brand manager. By the time she moved, she'd have three years of experience and could be making six figures easily.

"What are your thoughts on possibly moving here next year at the end of your lease?" I began the conversation with as much tentativeness as I could. The whole goal was to show Aaliyah that our relationship was a top priority above other major items in my life. I didn't want to offer any ultimatums or come off as self-centered.

"I'll consider it, but why can't you just move back to Flor-ida? You'll have a year's worth of work experience, so it'll be much easier for you to find a job back here. I don't even think I'll like it there at all," she replied back. This was a question I didn't prepare for and had no rehearsed answer. Not one thought crossed my mind that this would be an option for us. In my narrow point of view, I never considered moving back. "I don't want to live in Florida again. I've been here my whole life. You witnessed firsthand just how much I struggled to get a job. Plus look at it this way, in fairness, you've never actually been in this environment long enough to pass judgment on it," I rebutted firmly.

It would be these words, my own words, which I would attribute to my own demise with the love of my life.

Words that I began to regret
Words that echoed in the back of my mind
Words I held over my head for too long
Words that kept me from interacting with any other women
Words robbing me of my sanity

The conversation would end by her saying, "We'll just have to pray about it." Immediately, I thought to myself that I needed to verify with someone I trusted and whose opinion I valued that I wasn't being irrational here. First person who came to mind was Kendrick. He was someone I respected above all things because he wasn't going to just agree with me due to our friendship, but he'd point out the flaws I presented, in hopes to help me grow. His logic would be accompanied by reasoning and examples to help reinforce the points he was making. The outside point of view that was unbiased is what he represented, and I trusted his guidance in these types of situations.

"Ish, that was mad selfish of you to say you don't want to live in Florida again. You have to think about the love she has for her career and the proximity to her family with whom she is extremely close. And for you to say that had to inflict feelings of doubt about your willingness to see past Ismael and to see Ya'll as a whole. You need to apologize! And honestly, it's to early too even start having these conversations; you just moved, and you're creating unnecessary uneasiness between the two of you. Just chill. You guys will be fine. Trust me."

After hanging up with him, it really resonated just how self-centered I must have sounded to Aaliyah. *How dumb could I be?* I thought to myself. The whole purpose of the conversation was not to demonstrate any selfishness. And what did I do as soon as I was presented with a response I didn't prepare for? Panic and to give in to my own wants. She was too valuable for me to act this way. This night would be the first of many sleepless nights. Rem sleep would desert me like a bastard child left at the doorsteps of an orphanage by unloving, selfish parents.

"I got to apologize first thing in the morning. Maybe the damage wasn't as bad as I think. Crisis management is a must," my thoughts rested on the simplistic notion that an apology was a fix-all serum. I believed in my ability to effectively manipulate words in any conversation to convey sincerity or any emotion I wanted to replicate.

It was 7:03am the next day, and it was time to get in front of this situation before it got any bigger. "Good morning, Sweetie. First and foremost, I want to apologize to you about last night. I was beyond wrong by saying I didn't want to stay in Florida again. Location is irrelevant to me as long as you're there with me. I am not married to this area or anywhere else. My focus remains on what's best for us, so again I apologize." Just as I expected, she thanked me for recognizing my fault and proceeded to converse with me as we normally did. Aaliyah was blessed with a heart of pure gold. She had the ability to overlook the bad in any situation and truly seek out the greatness hidden behind one's malicious ways. So for me, my expectation was predicated on her employing her gift over belief in my worthless apology.

This was a trait I admired about her. It drew me to her, knowing there are humans out there who aren't so pessimistic and know deep down we are all capable of good. Her positivity was so infectious, even to someone like me who feared attachment to people due to the evil they may not even commit. She leveled me out, challenging my understanding of people—a concept I continuously struggled with, even till this day.

Aaliyah didn't ask me for much, aside from me taking the initiative in planning activities for us to do. All she wanted was for me to plan dates and outings for us. But I fed her the poor excuse of "I'm a homebody. I don't know what you want to do. Just tell me." When, in reality, I was too broke to pay for anything. It hurt having her pay for me. It messed with my manly identity. During this time, I was an unemployed college graduate with nothing but her love to keep me afloat.

She encouraged me that the right position was coming, but I kept dismissing her ways to uplift my spirits. I was too consumed with my realities to be a loving boyfriend. I skipped group outings from embarrassment, and I was too ashamed to communicate these things to her because I had done it so frequently. She was a blossoming flower, sunbathing in the glories of life while I was poison to her roots and draining her. I wanted to do for her because it was what I was supposed to do. Part of me didn't blame her for wanting to leave me. It was the best thing for her to do. I felt as if I had nothing to provide. No security to give. I was a waste of her time. Not to mention, once before I had taken advantage of her heart by cheating on her a year ago.

By making the decision to step outside our relationship, I embarrassed her. I broke the circle of trust we had built over time. Like the old saying goes, "What you do in the dark always comes to light." It proved to be true. There was no hiding or lying my way out of this one. I was guilty and there was no way I'd be proven innocent. I watched as the truth of who I really was pummeled her.

There was nothing for me to say to reassure her it was a mistake never to happen again. That could have been the end of our story, but she took me back against all fair warnings—parents, friends nor close confidants were in favor of us being together. But after much effort on my behalf to prove to her I was worth the time, she gave me a second chance. It took months of being apart for us to reconvene our relationship. I showed up to her job one day with flowers in hand as a surprise, sent edible arrangements. I did everything I could to demonstrate humility. I respected her for being able to forgive and forget my past transgressions. Aaliyah not once threw things in my face when disagreements arose. Her bravery to reintroduce me to her family as her boyfriend spoke volumes to me.

Aaliyah fought for this relationship to work on multiple occasions, but I kept failing. I blamed myself for losing her. I figured, in time, I'd heal because time healed all things. But that wasn't true. I would learn that healing is a three-step process. First, I had to forgive myself for the wrong I'd done and the lack of effort I demonstrated throughout our entire relationship. Then I had to forgive her for doing what was, ultimately, best for both of us. I needed to be alone to finish working on myself. My growing pains were hindering my way of thinking, and my negative mindset wasn't enjoyable to be around. Second, I had to decompress. During this time, I had to reflect on where I went wrong, what I could have done better, and how I could use this relationship as a platform for my next. Third, time—time would allow me to sort out my feelings, giving me the ability to recover from the shock of being without her. The collaboration of these three steps are what constitutes proper healing.

Aaliyah changed my life in a multitude of ways. She helped me re-establish my relationship with God. This woman did not play any games about me going to church. I was no stranger to my faith, but there was definitely a disconnect since leaving home for college. As a teenager, I went in order to appease my mother—more so than to gain fulfillment of the Body of Christ. By observing her commitment to Christianity—from attending services, serving in the children's ministry, down to her tithing—it showed me I had a long way to go in my faith. I was living with one foot in the world the other foot in the church. I never viewed myself as a heathen of any sort, but I knew I was a long way from being a model believer. I thank her for being that example, sparking what was instilled in me as a child. My faith was rejuvenated. The messages given at church had a whole new meaning as I connected to each and finding ways to apply the lessons in my own life. I was a reclaimed soul.

Her compassion for family was an ideal I found difficult to understand. Aaliyah was the only girlfriend I had who came from a strong family foundation. Both parents were active in her life, her biggest supporters. The Harrisons gave me a glimpse of the type of family I wanted to head one day. When Aaliyah was facing a tough decision, they would have conference calls to discuss viable options. Initially, I thought it was a joke as I was someone who made his own decisions and rarely consulting anyone, let alone my parents. Guess it stemmed from my arrogance of wanting to take on life by myself as if I had all the answers. Or maybe it was my ignorance of knowing the questions I had were askable. The Harrison's closeness was rewarding, even to a non-member of the family. They showed me how to celebrate family, shield one another's mistakes, and laugh while doing so.

She also showed me I was capable of giving love. For her, I'd give my left arm, not even thinking twice about it. Aaliyah broke down my selfish walls from time to time. I wanted to be selfless for her happiness. This selflessness was what every woman prior to her wanted, but she was the only one who could bring it out of me. Being the reason she smiled—one of her best assets—gave me purpose. I remember on her 24th birthday not having any money to do something for her. I humbled myself and asked Curtis for a small loan. Never in a million years would I have done that for anyone else, not even myself. But in that moment, I didn't care how I looked or felt about asking another man for money. My only concern was seeing her smile.

For Aaliyah, I have no ill will in my heart, but an appreciation for all she's done. As I am more honest with myself currently, I can say that I wouldn't be the person I am if it had not been for her. I am very grateful for the lessons in love and in companionship.

MASTERS IN UNEMPLOYMENT
WITH A PHD IN DEPRESSION

THE ENEMY: *As a black man, it was only fitting that I enter into a life of crime. I was born angry, aggressive and an animal! I was suited for the street life—no ties and slacks but ski masks and crack. So education or not, no one would hire me and I would die in prison by the hand of another inmate or by my own hand from continuous depression. Statistics proved there were more African-American males on prison yards than on illustrious college campuses across America. Who are you to think any different, nigga?!*

"ISH-MALE RA-SH-EED BROWN, "THE GRADUATION M.C. ANNOUNCED. A moment of bliss flooded my body. I conquered the realm of an undergraduate degree. I remember the days when this was a figment of my imagination. This wasn't a precedent set before in my family. There was now one to gaze upon in admiring fashion. I was the first male on both sides of my family to graduate from college. All I wanted to do was celebrate this timeless moment—then I remembered I had yet to secure a marketing job.

Granted, I was extended a few offers that were outside of my field of study, but I rejected them all. The reason was I wanted to find happiness in my employment. Growing up, I watched my mother work a job she despised for more than 20 years. Through her experience, I felt a sense of responsibility to my younger sibling and to me to go after what I wanted versus settling for a paycheck earned without passion. I valued my happiness more than money at this point. After analyzing the situations of all my peers, most of them settled—thoroughly hating going to work. I began to question what it was they feared when it came to obtaining the job they desired.

I knew once I vowed to go after what I wanted, I was in for the battle of my life. So it was me against a new enemy, a stronger, more challenging enemy—the competitive and, at times, impossible Real World! This enemy was by far more experienced and advanced than I was. This nemesis had joined forces with a few allies: bills, student loans, and a shaky job market. I approached this battle with an array of inadequate skills: confidence in self, an extended network, and faith in God's favor to provide me with what I needed.

> BOOM cracked the first shot! As I opened my eyes, I realized I was on the front line of this war. My heart pounded like an 808 drum, my palms sweated profusely, and my breathing—borderline, yielding an asthmatic collapse. Looking around, I could only see shadow-like figures of soldiers running to get in formation, those with rank shouting orders, and the bright hues of sunshine being escorted away by clouds of smoke from gun powder, grenade residue, and burning trees. Tears began to fill my eyes, but I honestly couldn't tell you if it was

from the burning sensation caused by the smoke in the air or the thought of dying on this battlefield. A fiery aroma filled the air, piercing my lungs as I inhaled with each breath. The deafening sound of .223 and .556 bullets exiting gun barrels penetrated my eardrums, followed by, "Die you cocksuckers," and "Mag out." Then what appeared to be my commanding officer vehemently blurted, "Private Brown, get your ass up and at em!"

It was May 5th, the first Monday after graduation, and I was down from my celebration high, and so disgruntled by the fact I had to go to work at a place that I had little to no interest in—Statewide Truck Leasing.

I began working at Statewide in January 2014, and God knows how much I needed the money. I was entering the last semester of my collegiate career and my financial situation was nothing short of tragic. I remember sitting at home over Christmas break 2013 not knowing where January rent money would come from.

My parents had over extended themselves financially, so I couldn't get it from them. *Where was I supposed to turn to?* It was times like this I would reflect on life and become overtaken by anger. I wanted the ability to stand on my own, depending on no one else but me. I was full of pride, yet too stubborn to ever ask for help. It was a sure sign of weakness and an inadequacy of self. I was firm in my belief that if I couldn't do it or find a way, then it couldn't be done. I was 23 years old, feeling as if all this holding out my hand was a direct result of my inabilities to provide for myself. I supported my irrational thinking with a verse from 2 Thessalonians 3:10 KJV: *"For even when we were with you, this we commanded you, that if any would not work, neither should he eat."* My personal interpretation of this verse would plague me for the duration of my teenage and early adult years. To me that verse meant *"If you don't work, you don't deserve to eat or even consider yourself a man, you might as well be dead out here."*

Unfortunately, I had to borrow the money from my line brothers. Should I be happy to have people who had the resources to bail me out? Of course, however, there was no relief. This was just placing a Band-Aid over a bullet wound. I lacked the essence of community and the ability to share my pitfalls with others. My personal life was a secret I was ready to take to the grave with me. Trusting others with my dark or embarrassing moments wasn't who I was. In retrospect, I feared more what people would do with this type of knowledge or what they would think of me.

After accepting the Statewide job, I knew life was on the up. Now I just had to focus on graduating then securing a career-building job in marketing. This company did more than rent moving trucks to household customers. They earned a bulk of their revenue from long-term leasing to companies. I literally had little to no knowledge of their business model or how the big bucks were made. Honestly, it didn't matter as long as I was able to get my check every Friday. This was temporary, so I just wanted to do what I had to.

My first week was your typical sit down talks with upper management to ease you into your position and welcoming you into the company. *"Ismael, we are looking for you to work anywhere from 30-40 hours a week,"* the District Rental Manager said. "I know you're in school, so just let us know what days you have classes, and we'll work around those times. We see the value in the skillset you bring to Statewide, so we want you to see the same value in our company for your future. This is a place where we could transition you into a post-graduation position. Ismael, trust me. We'll welcome you with open arms." They were thoroughly impressed by my abilities to speak, holding intellectual conversations. It was a perfect fit for the role of rental representative. The job description detailed that I would be interacting with customers constantly and answering phones pretty much all day. *This is easy. Talking to people is what I do.* I thought to myself about the role. Being naïve and broke, I jumped at the idea to work that many hours while going to school and being a student leader. *Cake, cake…did I mention more cake?* I thought. My schedule consisted of working on Mondays, Wednesdays, Fridays, Saturdays and Sundays; Tuesdays and Thursdays were reserved for classes.

At first, I actually liked the job. The level of complexity was there, and the people were extremely forthcoming in teaching me things. Originally, no one barked at me for being incompetent on how to do certain tasks. My coworkers actually took the time to walk me through the processes. The location in Orlando was the second busiest counter in the entire company; only second to the Las Vegas district office. I took pride in working in such a high-traffic environment—the possibility of building my arsenal of skills was all I could ask for. For a minute, I actually considered working there after graduation. It had absolutely nothing to do with my major, but the job security was there and the money was okay, at best. I was on the verge of settling early in the process of my job hunt. Like many other college students approaching graduation, I was scared of what was to come after walking across that stage, and this was my way out.

> The sun was setting behind the horizon, but there wasn't much sunshine to miss. I fell in line with my platoon where no one said a word. Everyone marched in silence. I couldn't even begin to form words from my mouth, so I followed suit.

> "We're going to set up a perimeter here. Comms go set up base one click east. Give me two snipers, one on each end of this terrain. Everyone else, check your gear. We're in for one hell of a firefight," barked out my commanding officer. You two privates are on the first watch. Keep your damn eyes open! He signaled to the soldier standing on my left and me. I couldn't make out his name or face at the time; nightfall had drowned out the possibility

of any visual confirmation. By now, my nerves had calmed somewhat, and I was yet to fire my weapon. Never had I considered killing a man; still unsure if I could. All of this was a freight train hitting me at once.

As I took my post, I stood there thinking about my family. I reached inside of my uniform to find a picture of them—but there was none. Then I remembered how badly I treated them before I left. I abandoned them all. My disappointments with life and myself blinded me to how much I needed them. I neglected to call, text, or even check in on my sister who was becoming a young woman. As my guilt began to build, I thought, "Damn, I ain't no good for…" Pwwwwwn—a bullet piercing the air sounded, connecting with the brain tissue of the solider standing not even a foot away from me.

His body hit the ground instantly. I froze in shock, not even acknowledging that the blood on my face was not my own. Everything stopped! I couldn't hear. My brain couldn't send any signals to the rest of my body.

This was my first true encounter with corporate America—from the politics of who should be promoted and when, to seeing the toll it took on over-worked employees, to the brutal unhappiness some employees couldn't hide. I just couldn't comprehend the number of miserable people at work around me. Thinking to myself, *How could you commit so much time to something that you ultimately dislike or that causes you to carry stress into other segments of your life?* But still, I remained there against my own views. I sold myself on the idea of staying there just for the summer, saving my money until I came across a better opportunity.

Under my rental lease, I had until August 16 to be out. That was my ultimate deadline to find the job I desired. Summer was the time not to go get it but to go take it. My resume had gone through several facelifts, visually and conceptually. The pressure was on because if I didn't lock in something by the end of my lease, then it was off to the military. Going back home was never an option. My pride wouldn't let me go back to my parents' house and live off them again.

What kind of example would I be setting for my sister?
How could I be any better than Dad, going back to live with my mother?
I looked down on him for being a grown man living with his.
All that hard work I put into college. Was it really for nothing?
God, what am I doing wrong?

So I decided to stay in Orlando until I got a job, no matter how long it took. I ended up selling all of my furniture to give me some financial comfort and took a bulk of my possessions back to Jacksonville. As far as living arrangements, I looked to those who didn't mind an extra body around the house temporarily. It was frustrating not having my own. The helplessness really impacted my view of myself. I felt weak, questioning my own identity as a man having to depend on someone else for shelter.

You are worthless, can't even afford your own place.
Man, you're 23 years old with nothing to show for it, and now you're at the mercy of some else's decision to tolerate your inability.
A man?
Naw, you ain't nothing, nowhere close.
You ought to be ashamed of yourself.
What would your sister think about you now?

Pride collided with humility. I began to distance myself from people. I was too ashamed to discuss the uncertainty of my future. As someone who had achieved so many accolades in college and as the one who "had" all of the answers when questioned about next steps in life, the pressure was now paralyzing.

May sped past. June began and ended. It was now July—nothing was materializing on the job search. Statewide was the only company in my corner, ready to coach me up the ladder. The choice was mine to drink the Kool-Aid and accept the job. By the end of July, I set my sights on getting to Houston. Everything was bigger in Texas, including the job market. I operated under the assumption that Houston was where I needed to be. The city was full of life, a relatively affordable cost of living, and it had a rising young black professional demographic. I had absolutely no factual evidence to accompany my logic, but at the time it sounded like the best viable option. I knew a few people there already, so it was a no-brainer. I carefully plotted a way to land in Houston.

I searched Statewide's company job portal, looking for manager-in-training openings in or around the Houston area. This role was designated for recent college graduates, so there weren't many years of experience required. It didn't take me even 10 minutes to discover the branch office in Houston had just one opening. I immediately scheduled a meeting with my supervisor to ask him to reach out to the Houston location on my behalf. This was one thing I was sure would work, and it did. The Houston office offered me the job and agreed to cover the truck rental to move. But what they didn't know was I planned on using them to get to Houston, working there only until I got a job I wanted.

I figured this way I'd make the best of my current offerings. So I went ahead and put in my two-weeks notice to secure the offer. My decision was made privately without consulting Aaliyah, who would be affected gravely. I was apprehensive to have the conversation with her, but it was inevitable that we discuss it. I neglected to allow her in on my thought process. She could have provided much desired insight and encouragement to keep my faith high. It was cowardice on my part when I should have affirmed her contribution to the decision, demonstrating the qualities of a great companion—more importantly, those of a man.

To take my mind off my reality, I counted down the days until my getaway to Toronto, Ontario. Kendrick had put this whole trip together with a couple of his friends who were Toronto natives, Daniel and Marcus. Daniel was a colleague of Kendrick's. The two of them met during their time as interns one summer in New York. Marcus was the childhood friend of Daniel who would come to the states to party with his buddy. The three of them had stories for days about their nights out. I was just happy to get invited.

Kendrick and I were going to Toronto for Drake's October's Very Own Festival. As a huge Drake and music fanatic all around, the entire week was bound to be a euphoric experience. This trip would prove to be more than a vacation. It became the reminder I needed, reinforcing why I was holding out for a job in my field. I'd come to the decision to postpone the conversation with Aaliyah until after my trip. I prioritized my own fun over what I needed to handle in talking to Aaliyah.

Toronto—commonly coined by names like TDot or The 6—was magnificent.

The people were oddly friendly. The air was fresh and clear in the summer. What more could anyone ask for? As a first time visitor, I quickly learned just how diverse and culturally infused the people of Toronto were. At first glance, I couldn't decipher between who was white, black, Asian or of Caribbean descent. This melting pot of culture produced a plethora of dialects, accents, foods, and looks—all united behind the scarlet maple leaf of Canada. Never before had I experienced so many varieties of people in one concentrated area. It was culturally shocking, but I took in every moment with full enjoyment.

Daniel and Marcus proved to be excellent hosts. They rolled out the red carpet for Kendrick and me. They provided us with recommendations for a number of food spots, and even listed dishes that we couldn't leave without trying. My favorite of all happened to be a Canadian staple, *poutine*. This dish was a heart attack in a bowl, ready to dangerously clog the arteries of everyone brave enough to consume it. The basis of poutine consists of crispy french fries covered in savory brown gravy, topped with piping hot, melting cheese curds. The experience was a party in my pallet. "Man, we should bring this to the states, immediately," I said with obvious fat-boy excitement. The two of them took me to my first Major League Baseball game at the Rogers Centre, where the Toronto Blue Jays played, and it was exhilarating. I wasn't the biggest fan of baseball, yet I was still knowledgeable of the sport, just not a huge viewer of games on television. But in person, it was a totally different experience. Everything from the fans angrily screaming at the umpire's bad call on a pitch to doing the wave with nearly 40,000 other people in attendance. It was magical.

Kendrick and I were there for close to a week, just exploring The 6. We were true tourists, taking to the streets in the daytime, just exploring the heart of downtown Toronto. I took over 300-plus pictures with my d3200 Nikon of vibrant street art, fellow streetwalkers, and traffic signage. I snapped still images of everything because I never wanted to forget this place. An affinity for Toronto grew deep inside during the course of my visit. The city was welcoming beyond measure. It amazed me by having much more to offer than what I was able to take in during my stay.

Returning back to the States, I felt rejuvenated and ready to attack these job applications without mercy. Especially, if I ever wanted to return to The 6, I needed a job to fund the trip. Upon arriving, I was greeted by Aaliyah, to whom I owed a difficult conversation that I had been withholding from her. We both were elated to see each other. I missed her and there was no secret about that.

I contemplated telling her my plans over dinner that night, but I retreated in fear yet again. I wouldn't get around to that conversation until a few days later after church. I went over to her place with nothing more than an ounce of courage. "So sweetie, I want to tell you something slash talk to you about something," I began timidly.

"Statewide offered me the management trainee position in Houston and…I accepted. I'm not completely sold on the position at all. You know I really don't like Statewide anyway, let alone moving so far just to do the same thing for such a small salary. I accepted it because I didn't have anything else and my lease is ending, so I had to do something." She looked at me with an empty stare. I knew the thought of me leaving wasn't appealing to her by any measure. I continued explaining my thought process behind my decision, "Aaliyah, I can't go home. My people already got their own financial issues. I'm not going back just to be a burden. Right now, it's either take this job or begin the onboarding process for the military." Before I could go on, the tears came running down my face. I was overwhelmed with emotion and was conflicted. Truthfully, I can admit I didn't want to leave her. But I knew being in Houston could open many doors of opportunity for me.

"Ish, don't feel pressured to accept this role just because it's all you have. You don't have to settle, but you do need to be positive and let your faith go before you. You must remain patient until the position you want comes," she said holding tears herself. She was by far more hopeful than I ever was during this time of uncertainty. Her strength was encouraging. It amazed me how confident in her faith she was. I took her advice, deciding to stick it out unaware of how long this could take or how challenging being unemployed would be.

July was no more. August arose and descended like the sun. It was now September with zero job offers. By now, I was out of my apartment, starting to lie about where I was living to everyone who asked—and still unemployed. "Just stay positive. It will happen as long as you believe it," I told myself time and again and again. By this time, I had now been out of a job going on three weeks, needing to cover my phone bill, gas, and food.

Jimmy Mann, one of my Bible study leaders, committed his life to doing God's work and blessing people in anyway he could. He did just that for me by connecting me with a fellow church member at Orlando World Outreach Church, where I had started attending service. Jimmy put me in contact with a school district employee who was looking to fill a role at Freedom Middle School for an after school Boys & Girls Club program. I was more than willing with nothing to lose and only money to earn. I figured it would be easy and temporary.

Gregory Mason, the fellow church member and school district employee of Orange County, was more than supportive of me filling the role. It was really the first victory I'd received since graduating in May. It was a moment to be thankful for, but still not what I ultimately wanted, so I reframed from any premature celebrations.

Working with middle school kids couldn't be that bad, right?
I was still relatively young and could relate to them.
Kids loved me.

I thought I was cool, and this would be easy money. It didn't even take two weeks for me to discover how wrong I was. These kids were at the stage in life where they felt the need to prove they weren't kids anymore but couldn't decipher between acting their age or being too grown. They exhibited a disregard for authority from anyone who wasn't their teacher. I felt the need to provide them with some guidance and mentorship. I reflected on the role of mentors in my life and the value of the lessons they instilled in me. I kept an open mind when dealing with insubordinate teens. Under the direction of Gregory, our program leader, I was assigned the sports activity. This was the most desired activity there was within the whole program. Once the activity cards were placed on the lunch tables, those kids swarmed like bees on honeycombs.

"You'll be fine. They don't bite," Gregory said jokingly, but I didn't see any humor in that statement at all. Brandon, another newly hired staffer, whom I also recognized from church, escorted what seemed like 100-plus kids over to the gym.

There was absolute chaos as soon as we released the balls to them. "Man, these kids are juiced on all types of sugar," I said to Brandon.

"Boy, you ain't never lied," he replied. Brandon was someone I learned a lot from. I related to him in multiple ways. He was older and more experienced in life than I was. Funny how the cards of life were dealt because we were in the same position, both looking for full-time roles to make us happy. He was someone who was proud of his journey in life and harbored no shame for his mistakes. He was open with his testimony and his walk with God, something I wasn't too sure where I stood. Brandon and I would encourage each other throughout the duration of our employment at the Boys & Girls Club program at Freedom Middle School.

Another month passed by and still not a single offer for a job. I was reaching my breaking point. I had been fasting all summer, praying, reading my Bible, but not a single *yes* from any of the positions I'd applied for. My faith was withering like an unwatered rosebud; it was slowly dying. My whole life, I believed all it took was to have faith the size of a mustard seed to move a mountain or to part the Red Sea, but not in my case. I felt as if faith the size of an elephant wouldn't help me get hired.

It was now October 2014, my birth month, a time when I really didn't feel any joy, only more disappointment. But girlfriend and best friend Aaliyah was there with me throughout this entire process. She was my rock, a positive foundation that I needed day in and day out. She endured more than she should have throughout our relationship. But during this time, I'll never forget the support she provided me. For my birthday, she made me feel special with her thoughtfulness. She gave me a reason to smile. I felt guilty for being so negative, but it was my only way to communicate how severe my situation was.

That evening we went to Eddie V's Prime Seafood, an elegant candle-lit restaurant with succulent menu choices—perfect for romantic dates. Aaliyah was beautiful in her red evening dress that she wore just for me. We actually matched that night, and we were beyond fly. Turning heads from the time we pulled up to the valet. I wore a red European-cut blazer with black trimming on the lapels with slim cut grey slacks ending off with black Cole Haan loafers—no socks, of course. Everything about the night just felt right. I didn't think once of being unemployed. We elected to sit next to each other, enjoying the comfort of proximity. Dinner was full of laughs and full of positive energy. I needed a timeout from life and to celebrate myself thus far. Aaliyah really helped me do that. This night was the push I needed to get refocused on finding a job.

In the next phase of my job search, I became more aggressive in tapping into my extensive network.

> *All these people I know, man, somebody can help me get a job easily.*
> *I should have been blowing up phone logs and email inboxes.*

At this point, I put my faith in people more than anything else. Through the course of my collegiate career, I served in several leadership roles, especially within my fraternity, where I shook hands and exchanged greetings with earth shakers. These were men who garnered influence throughout corporate America and within their respective communities. I had come across men working in all industries from engineers at Lockheed Martin to lobbyists on Capitol Hill to successful self-employed businessmen.

During my senior year, I held the highest position in my fraternity that an undergraduate member can hold, the Assistant Regional Vice President of the Southern Region. I figured I had nothing to lose, only the world to gain, in this position with opportunities spanning from public exposure, uncapped networking, and professional development. This role looked even better on a resume, so it was an easy decision to take the time to focus on bettering myself. Stepping into the role, I expected doors to automatically open for me. I assumed that brothers would be forthcoming with postgraduate opportunities.

I'll easily get a job. I can finally relax. A bruh will definitely look out for me.

Was I wrong? No, not at all. It was the premise on which our organization was built, brotherhood. I was amiss in thinking these brothers owed me anything. My mindset was the issue here. Relationship building was key to gaining any assistance in life versus just walking around filled with expectations. People in general were more susceptible to helping those they knew on a personal level.

I would approach brothers with charisma in my voice and genuineness in my plea for help. In my speeches I delivered, I would emphasize the importance of older brothers reaching back, guiding the generations behind them, for our society depended upon it. They loved it. I took pride in being transparent with my lack of certainty after graduation. Just like with any other people in life, there were brothers who said they would and didn't but also those who offered and followed through.

Former General President Jullian Davis, Sr. was one who kept his word. His son, Jullian, Jr., worked at HighTech in its legal department in Mountain View for about two years. "Brother Brown, my son works at HighTech. I'll connect you with him and stay on him about helping you out. Hell, you'll be helping him, too. If you get hired, he'll get a referral stipend if I'm not mistaken. What's your field of study?" he concluded.

That following Monday morning, I received an email from Jullian Davis, Jr. in which he introduced himself, his expectations, and his "don't waste my time" demeanor. I was receptive of everything he spelled out. I figured he knew exactly what HighTech wanted in new hires. JD, as he was also known, took his time in further vetting me, ensuring he wasn't putting his name on someone incompetent. Through an exchange of nearly 20 email correspondences, JD became very familiar with my background after examining my resume and providing feedback to help improve the quality of it. At the same time, he also walked me through the HighTech onboarding process, taking his time to communicate just how difficult and time consuming the entire cycle can be. JD was very transparent. For that I appreciated him. I was in no place to be impatient or attempting to dictate terms. All of his resume feedback I applied without rebuttal. He works there; *he knows exactly what these people are looking for. Just do whatever he says.* I trusted him and totally believed he had my best interest in mind. With his referral, I knew at least an interview was an easy lock.

Two weeks passed—and nothing. I prayed extensively for this one opportunity to actually happen for me. I just knew God had my back on this.

> Lord, I know I'm not your best son but a son nonetheless. I am on my knees asking for a breakthrough. You know my heart, and you see how much I need this, Lord. Getting hired by HighTech can change my whole family's life. Having that name alone on my resume can propel me to heights I never imagined. But I know through you, Lord, it's possible.

You said in your Word in 2 Corinthians 5:7, "walk
by faith and not by sight." So I am entrusting that
what I cannot see will be bestowed upon me as a
believer and doer of your Word. In Your son Jesus'
name I pray. Amen.

Not even a day after I said that prayer came an email from a
HighTech recruiter. This email gave me a fresh understanding of the
true power or prayer. That email gave me a new sign of life. It gave
me hope that I could possibly be an asset to a company. I opened
that email with a smile on my face because I knew it was going to be
an outline as to what steps were next. But unfortunately, it was yet
another rejection letter.

Everything on which I was raised conflicted with my current
situation. I questioned God when I was taught never to do so. I was
falling into the depths of depression, becoming a stranger to hope
and more familiar with negativity. I was convinced my prayers were
falling on deaf ears and that someone who had God's ear was praying
against me.

God, why won't you help me?
Haven't I been through enough?
Everyone around me is getting the jobs and the answers they
need.
Why can't I?
Am I not saying the right words in my prayers?
Why won't you say anything?

I just couldn't wrap my head around the rejection. I felt as if I had
put in the time and effort necessary to become an ideal candidate for
any company. Education, experience, and even leadership roles—I
thought I had it all. I even took it a step further by creating a documentary series titled *More Than A Student*.

More Than A Student (MTAS) turned out to be one of my better ideas, but it was poorly executed. The original vision for MTAS was to motivate everyday college students to become more than just students, taking on new challenges, getting involved, and easing the transition from college classrooms to corporate boardrooms. Creators Deshaun Artis, Melissa Houlemarde and me felt the need to encourage our peers all over the nation, across all university campuses, to unlock the visionary within them. We understood the significance of sacrifice, living it daily through our involvement in organizations or other extracurricular activities. Deshaun and I decided to record everything we were a part of outside the classroom for the duration of the 2013–2014 school year. We agreed to release a new episode every other week with Melissa narrating each. She would also run our social media outlets. It sounded like a sure fire hit series, giving a face and personality to leadership. At the time, the only thing on TV or online that appealed to our generation were reality shows making everyday imbeciles into stars. It was pure trash dumbing down the minds of all those who viewed them. MTAS was going to break the cycle and empower youth.

But as a graduating senior living the life of more than a student, the series flopped. We all fell victim to our super-involved lifestyles. Time was a commodity none of us had enough of. The series, if you can even characterize it as such, only saw the creation of two episodes and a few article blog posts. It was disappointing, but I still could see the value in what we created and all the additional footage still unreleased. For me, this documentary series served a dual purpose. It was a visual resume, giving employers examples of my abilities in action and how I could handle a multitude of things all at once. This series was my secret weapon when speaking with interviewers.

But none of it worked. It all seemed to be a waste of time. I was continuously losing with each application submitted—receiving *no* after *no*. The rejection emails poured in by the tens daily. They all conveyed the same generic message of *no, you're not good enough* but expressed in a variety of ways.

You had some companies that thanked you for your time, even encouraging you to try applying again in the future.

> Thank you so much for giving us the opportunity to consider you for employment. Your interest in our company means a lot. We've reviewed your application and, unfortunately, it's not a match for what we're specifically looking for this time around.
>
> We know it takes a lot to submit an application, so we want you to know how much we truly appreciate you doing so! If you see a new role later down the line, please don't hesitate to apply again.
>
> We wish you all the best.

Then you had other companies that cared less if you came back to their company looking for employment.

> Thank you for expressing an interest in the Marketing Assistant position. While this has not been an easy decision, we have decided to consider other candidates.
>
> Again, thank you for taking the time to apply and pursue this position. We wish you the very best in your future career endeavors.

Oh, and my absolute favorite was when companies mentioned keeping you on file, promising to contact you if your qualifications matched a future job posting. But guess what? They never contact you—ever.

Thank you for your expressed interest for the position of Marketing Coordinator.

After careful consideration and representative of a very competitive marketplace, we regret to inform you that we are unable to move you forward in the process.

Your information will remain active in our system, and if your skill set is identified as a potential fit for future opportunities, you will be contacted for further discussion. You can also set up alerts in your profile to notify you of new jobs that become available which match your interest and/or skill set.

Again, thank you for your interest.

It was a condescending way of communicating you're not good enough for their company and they felt sorry for you. It came to the point where I could recite the denial verbiage and would repeat it to myself, believing what they said. Again, I was losing. I began taking direction from my emotions, the absolute worse possible thing to do.

"BROWWWWWWN, get down dammit," my commanding officer belched from deep down in his soul, attempting to save my life. But I still couldn't move, my boots became cinder blocks as my knees locked up, and bullets continued to fill the night air whistling by. I could see the fallen soldier's blood soak the surrounding area where his body lay. The blood began to drown out the surrounding shrubbery and drain deep into the soil, softening the foundation we walked on.

Before I knew it, I was forced to the ground forcefully. Initially, I couldn't tell if a bullet had hit me and this was where I'd meet my maker, so I just closed my eyes, preparing myself. The only thing that reminded me that I was still alive was the warmth of another body and the stale dry breath blanketing the back of my neck.

Then he spoke, "Snap out of it, and get your sh*t together, soldier, or you will end up just like him." I opened my eyes and gazed over to the lifeless body that was still losing blood by the second. For a minute, I envied my dead comrade because he had been freed from the fear that fueled this war. It was fear that encouraged each participant to do what he or she must in order to make it home. That same fear that caused the shakiness in your hands to cease as an enemy crossed into your sights forcing your trigger finger to squeeze. The same fear that devoured the remorse you once felt for killing another human being. Fear was the ruler of these lands, and if you didn't own any of it, you were at a disadvantage.

My clouded judgment began to affect my decision-making. I was the senseless owner of a semi-automatic Mossberg .22 AR-15 with no state issued license to conceal. Purchased during the time when I worked for Statewide, there was a surplus of money, and I felt the need to own a gun. Owning a gun gave me the power to destroy any and all threats to my life. It was a form of protection against evil. But there was no protection from myself, someone under the impression that men owned guns. It was no different than owning a cell phone or having a driver's license.

Oh yea, this just what I needed right here.
Who want problems now?
Matter fact, who the punk now?
I can handle myself like a man.

Uneducated on gun safety or how to properly clean or even use the weapon, I was a danger to everyone around me. If anything, I was feeding into the stereotype I dared to escape. I was just another young unemployed black male in America, carrying an assault rifle illegally, awaiting trouble or a run-in with the police. And it didn't become illegal until I made the ill-advised choice to ride with it laid across my backseat. Not feeling of much worth, I guess in one way or another, I related to the stereotype. Being without a full-time job, reflecting on how worthless I felt, I could hear ScHoolboy Q's line from his song *Hoover Street* in my mind repeating again and again.

> *"Just brought a gun f*ck punching in…"*

The art of his wordplay painting his dismay for unemployment along with his acceptance of criminal activity—glorifying the violence he participated in while avoiding capture. It was his way of playing the cards he was dealt in life. Finding solace in his unfortunate circumstances, declaring himself a *real nigga, the product of a real nigga* and asking himself how did it feel to be a *real nigga*. The whole motivation behind his criminal endeavors was to obtain financial stability, something neither he nor I had at the time.

I didn't amount to anything because I knew better. I had a loaded 30-round clip in an AR-15 on my backseat. I truly had no intentions of committing any form of crime or hurting anyone. I was just stressing, diving deeper into depression. I searched for ways to justify my rationale for keeping it in the car because I didn't have a place of my own, so bringing it into someone else's home was inexcusable. At the time of purchase, I had my own apartment, keeping the rifle safely hidden. But 10 months later, living on the edge of homelessness, the car was the only place to store it.

No one knew what I was going through, which was also my fault. I had distanced myself from those who cared about me or were willing to lend an ear and give me some reassurance that everything would work out. Full of embarrassment, I dreaded answering the question, "What are you doing now since you graduated? " I had no answer. I was too prideful to tell the truth. I would either talk around the question or ignored the text messages that asked.

I was on a bad path. I wanted to hide from everyone, including those who thought highly of me. I felt I would let them down if I expressed myself. It held true one weekend when I went home to Jacksonville to absorb love from my family, and my sister asked to drive my car. I gave her the keys without thinking. Then I remembered the gun being across the backseat. "Monica, hold on. Let me grab some stuff out of there first," I blurted out nervously.

"I can grab it. Just let me know what you need out of there," she replied. Her innocence and unselfishness just wanted to help out her big brother. But I couldn't allow her to see what her big brother really was—a disappointment facing 20-plus years in prison if pulled over.

"No, I'll get it. Thank you, though," I stated while trying to regain my calm composure. Like the angel she was, she listened and gave up. I proceeded to go outside, opening the rear door on the driver's side to retrieve the gun without being seen. And just as I'm coming through the front door, there's my mother ready to meet me. My whole body tensed up, frozen in place. I began to pant as it became harder to breathe. The rifle was stored in a box undetectable by the naked eye, but my mom was an officer. She always asked the questions—the right questions.

"What's that, Boop?" she asked as she examined the box. I knew the brand name of the rifle was on the exterior of the box, so I couldn't do nothing but tell the truth. I swallowed the oversized lump in my throat and spoke timidly. All that toughness I had when buying it and riding around my car with was gone. "It's a gun, mom," I replied.

I truly believe she asked only to see if I would lie to her because she didn't show any immediate signs of disgust with me. I was utterly shocked, but I kept my composure. "Let me see it," she continued. I proceeded to lay down the box and unlatch the holding mechanism, keeping the rifle secure inside. Once unboxed, I went straight to disengaging the magazine, the one bullet in the chamber, and placed the safety on. I could feel her stares as she watched me handle the high-powered rifle. As an officer having to take frequent trips to the gun range to ensure her skills were up to par and being fully aware of safety measures when deploying her weapon, I feared what I knew was coming. "Son, aim it down. Treat it as if it's loaded at all times," she instructed.

That automatically let me know she didn't see me take the loaded mag out as I assumed she had. I was truly unsure how she could have missed anything at that point. I was briefly relieved until her next question came piercing through my ears. "Okay, now let me see your concealed carry weapons license, since you just riding around with a semi-auto in your car," she said calmly with a bit of attitude. My demise was quickly approaching, but there was no way I would make it out of this one unscathed.

"I don't have one," I acknowledged, contemplating whether or not I should have lied. But there was no lie to save me. Even if I had all day to devise a clever lie, there absolutely was none to tell. My chest pounded so ferociously that I'm almost positive my mother could see each heartbeat through my shirt. There was no explanation to provide. An apology wasn't applicable either. I was well aware of what I was doing but, nonetheless, it just wasn't my best moment

"Ismael," she began. She rarely ever said my name, so that was strike number one. "Do you know what kind of trouble you could get into? Like are you thinking? You can't be that stupid. There are cops out there looking to harass you, and you want to give them a reason to lock you up? What kind of example are you setting for your sister? Do you want to go back to jail?" She continued on, but my ears muted her. I couldn't take any more slandering because I knew what this did to her.

Hurting her was never an aim of mine. It was actually one of my greatest fears. All she ever wanted for me was to live out her teachings of being better than my surroundings and better than the men I watched while growing up. The ability to steer clear of the easy route out of difficult times by turning to crime, that's all she wanted for me. I was disappointing her and showing my inability to be resilient like she was my entire life. Weak, unworthy of her love, and a quitter is what I felt in that moment. I wasn't as strong as she was. It was evident through my actions.

She was right.
How could I be so dumb?
What was I going to do if the cops pulled me over?
Run?
I wasn't ready for the life that came with my decisions.
What do I say to let her know I'm not as stupid as I seemed right now?
I deserve the tongue-lashing she's whipping out right now.

As my ears reactivated, I heard her say, "Son, I know it's hard out there, and this was not what you were expecting after graduation, but this is inexcusable. Life has knocked you down plenty of times before and did it not work itself out? Have you forgotten everything you've been through? This is just another testament to God's ability to do exceedingly and abundantly in our lives. It is his will for you to go through this. He is trying to teach you something." I just couldn't understand.

I was broke. How could she not see that? Being broke is the equivalent to being dead. There's no other comparison that can encompass the emotional stress, depression, and hunger pains you feel when you're broke. I had a girlfriend whom I couldn't do anything for, a phone bill I was barely scraping up money to pay for, student loan payments pouring in, but she couldn't see that. I wanted to die.

There was nothing I desired more than for it all to end, freeing myself of all the crap I was dealing with. My life was full of struggles. Yes, but I had enough. I looked to the sky and yelled at God, "NO MORE! I can't take anymore." I could not make ends meet on my own, and it destroyed my manly identity. I would hear voices telling me to kill myself.

Get in that car, do about 80, and drive off the Dames Point Bridge.
Buy some Xanax pills and mix it with NyQuil. It'll take you under.
Overdose on them.
Just be a man.
Shoot yourself. It's quick and easy.
You won't feel anything.
Jump off the top of a garage building on UCF's campus.
Just do it.
Life ain't gone get any easier. Might as well check out now.
No one would miss you.

These thoughts I never shared with anyone, especially not my mother. I didn't know who to tell or even how to begin a conversation about wanting to kill myself. I loaded that rifle many of times and considered pulling the trigger. I placed the barrel under my chin, placing the butt of the rifle between my legs then closing my eyes.

Should I pray?
I don't even know what to say.
Should I write a goodbye letter?

Guess I'm going to hell.
It couldn't have been any worse than what I was living in.
I'd backstroked in the blue-flamed lake of fire.
Exchanged greetings with the demons that whispered to me in the dark.
This can't be how it's supposed to end.

My body temperature increased and my hands shook as I sat in the dark, contemplating my next moments. Breathing was extremely difficult. My lips trembled as I let out an overflow of tears. The voices returned, but this time yelling at me to do it.

What are you waiting on?
Get this over with already.
Oh, I get it, you can't do this either, huh?
Damn, you are super weak!

I dropped the rifle and began weeping on the floor. I thought about everything—from the impact my suicide would have on my sister, as she got older thinking that she wasn't there to save me; the impact on my mother, believing she failed as a parent when she absolutely didn't. All the people I'd made smile would be left with a million questions as to why. Some of them would have carried some blame, and they didn't deserve that because they actually loved me.

I thought back to Gerald and how he questioned life while I was being so judgmental. I wasn't any better than he was. I guess we heard the same voices trying to convince us to take the ultimate gift of life away. I denied myself the help I needed by keeping my mouth closed. I allowed fear of judgment and shame to obstruct my path of mental liberation. This was no one's fault but my own. I was surrounded by so many willing and able souls who would have given their last to help me through. I just robbed them of the opportunity to love such a negative doubt-filled Ismael.

I told my mother she was right in everything she was saying, but I omitted delving deeper into any more conversation before I started to tell her how I really felt. I would leave the rifle in her possession, rescuing me from any weapons charges.

Shifting my focus back to the soldier laying on top of me, it was a fellow solider from my platoon who risked his own life to ensure mine was still in tact. Before he rolled off me, he had given me orders to retrieve a few items off the body of our lifeless brother. "Go get his meds and dog tags, then we're going to carry him back to where comms set up," he said sternly. "We need to move fast, staying low to the ground before we join him in dog heaven," he continued. I gathered myself emotionally and slowly regained feeling back into my lower extremities. I began army crawling over to the body.

As I slowly approached the body, my training returned to me. As a bomb specialist, I knew what to look for when detecting mines or anything else that went BOOM. I finished top of my AIT class for assembling some of the deadliest explosives, neutralizing all in the vicinity. I analyzed the area, checking any land mines or signs of any other surprises from the enemy. Nothing appeared alarming in my search, so I positioned myself next to the body.

Lying directly in his pool of blood, I reached over to his vest and began my search for his meds. But before I could open any of the compartments of his vest, I came across his name patch and it read I. Brown. I thought maybe all the distress I was under caused me to hallucinate. I took a deep breath, exhaled, and wiped my face with my hands covered in bloody mud. I looked back at his name patch and again it read I. Brown. Coincidence? Maybe. So I reached for his dog tags, and they read Ismael Rashid Brown Jacksonville, FL. His tags were identical to mine! Then I looked up to what was left of his face. It was me…I was in this war, alone!

It all started to come full circle. It wasn't a coincidence that I was assigned to the bomb unit. I had been blowing up relationships around me my whole life.

Returning back to Orlando, the pressure to turn my situation around was even heavier because my mom had caught a glimpse of my depression. I began submitting even more applications. I utilized everything from Monster, Indeed, Glassdoor, LinkedIn and respective company sites. I wasn't going to allow any job requisites fitting what I was looking for in a company pass me by. By this time, I had also revamped my resume to give it visual pop with some color and unique placement of sections. In addition to a new resume, I also earned two online certifications: Google Adwords and Google Analytics. Now it was a matter of finding the ideal company. I required working for a company that promoted creativity, viewed personal development as a priority for young talent, and championed marketing to be something the employees lived.

For me, marketing existed in every aspect of life, branding most specifically. When pursing someone of the opposite sex, you put your best foot forward, selling him or her on your brand. Next comes communicating the brand being sold as a value proposition to them as consumers. Our personalities also serve as segments of our brand. They become walking, talking advertisements of self. The same principles apply when applying to jobs and wanting to impress employers. You ensure your brand aligns with that of the company's in order to demonstrate the value you can bring, therefore, enhancing their brand. The creativity to find innovative ways to sway people to buy into your brand is one of the most exciting thrills of life. It keeps you on your toes, constantly sharpening your skills. So if a company's employees didn't think this way, then there was no need for me to waste time, mine and the company's, interviewing.

But I can't lie. I wasted a lot of time being desperate for money. I was submitting applications and even interviewing for roles I knew weren't for me—going against my entire campaign of not settling. But I persevered. I officially became a member of Orlando World Outreach Church and realigned with what always pulled me through, God. Officially joining that church boosted my spirits, placing me around people who generally bubbled with positive energy, which I was empty on. Along with joining, I also began serving on the Parking ministry, greeting people as they pulled in and assisting them in finding a parking spot.

I needed to be rejuvenated, refueled and refocused on the teachings that I grew up on. You learn, as you get older, there are some things that never leave you because they are at the core of who you are. By doing this at a time when I had nothing else to try or give, the opportunities began pouring in. In March 2015, two companies demonstrated keen interest in my skillset and past experience. One was Action7, a world leading all-terrain footwear, apparel and equipment brand based in Southborough, Massachusetts, about 15 minutes outside of the Boston metropolitan area. I applied for the position of digital marketing associate. Through this role, I would be responsible for managing all social media handles, creating rich content to engage the target audience, and increasing brand awareness. This was something I had a wealth of knowledge in. My experience bled online engagement through several of the positions I'd held in the past. I was the perfect fit.

The other company was ABC Marketing Incorporated, a full-service marketing agency dedicated to growing membership for non-profit associations. This company was located in the heart of Old Town, Alexandria, Virginia, just right outside Washington, D.C. The position I applied for was for account coordinator, responsible for managing all marketing functions for assigned accounts requiring extensive consulting services and providing all necessary marketing counsel, budgeting, project management, program implementation and other related services. A position that I also felt well suited for.

Action7 was the first to reach out, asking me to do a routine phone interview with the marketing manager. After successfully making it through a gauntlet of phone interviews, I was asked to come into the office in Southborough for interviews with various team members with whom I may be working. I was excited and even more thrilled that they were forking up the funds to fly me out because I just couldn't afford the short notice flight.

Boston?
This could be my new home.
I am so close to getting a job I can taste it.
Lord, I hope I get this one.
You know how much I need this.

Stepping off the plane, I inhaled deeply, taking in the cold stiff Boston air. I exhaled any nervousness left in me. Mentally, I locked in and focused on what I'd come there to do, leave with a job. I had everything I needed—printed resumes, portfolio of sample digital campaigns I'd created or worked on, and even an additional presentation detailing the eight reasons I was a perfect fit. The creative presentation was my initiative to go the extra distance to show each interviewer that I was serious and meant business. Upon arriving, I was greeted at the entrance into the colorful, sneaker-filled office suite.

Anyone who knows me knows just how much I appreciate a nice pair of sneakers. Over the years, I built up quite the collection, ranging from Nikes basketball shoes from stars like LeBron James, Kobe Bryant, Kevin Durant and Michael Jordan. I took my footwork very seriously. To think a sneaker company could possibly employ me was surreal. I received an office tour in addition to a schedule of my day, which consisting of 4 interviews with the marketing manager, two directors, and the chief operating officer (COO).

One by one, I lined them up, knocking them dead with enthusiasm in my voice and associated stories to back up my response for each question they asked. They all left the interview room impressed and with smiles on their faces. Then came time to sit with the COO, who seemed very uninterested in the interview process. For him, I would have to step up the delivery of what I could bring to Action7. At the conclusion of our 20-minute discussion, he expressed his major concern with hiring me:

"I think you're bright, well accomplished, and possibly a great fit for the role. However, with you being in Florida, I'm not sure how comfortable I am uprooting you and having you move to Boston, which is incredibly expensive. That is really concerning because you would be starting in an entry-level role trying to navigate the big city." I went on to reassure him that relocating wasn't an issue because I had fraternity brothers in the area that I could stay with as I was transitioning. He nodded his head, smiled, and thanked me for my time. I left the Boston area feeling as if I locked it up without a doubt. But I couldn't count on it until there was an official offer.

I had very little time to focus on that interview because the very next day I had to interview with ABC. The initial interview wasn't your customary phone call. It was an actual Skype interview with the managing Director of Account Services. Basically, he was the head honcho of the department I was applying for. I approached this interview with the same confidence I had for the Action7 position. Talking to people wasn't an issue I had, so I always felt prepared.

This interview lasted no more than 30 minutes. He thoroughly enjoyed our conversation and asked me, "Why in the world do you want to leave sunny Florida and move to D.C.?" My answer was simple. "I understand there are greater opportunities outside of the state I've called home all my life, and I am ready to explore those options, " I replied.

And like that I had moved on in the process where I would Skype interview with other directors of the company. This stage consisted of four rounds of interviews. But they were no different in the appeal I presented to Action7. I had every intention to close out these interviews with an offer on the table. I had nothing else to lose. I had already been told no 331 times. I kept every single rejection email as a reminder of what I had been through. These emails were motivation to keep going and never forgetting those who told me I wasn't good enough.

It would take a week and a half after that week of eight rounds of interviews before ABC would offer me an opportunity. That's right. I got offered not just a job but also a career in marketing. This was something that I had held out for close to a year after graduating college. I received the offer letter via email at 10am on Wednesday April 15th. But I was required to return the offer, signed and by 4:30pm the same day. The pressure was on because I was still holding out for Action7 to render a decision on my candidacy. Out of the two positions, I wanted Action7 more because it involved working with sneakers, and I would be required to travel to headquarters in the United Kingdom. The travel alone was enticing enough for me to select Action7. Who didn't want to go to the U.K. on the company's dime for a week? This was one of my top five travel destinations. I was sold.

I emailed the marketing manager at Action7 immediately, informing her of the situation.

I just wanted to inform you that I've recently been offered another marketing position. My desire and true interest is to be an Action7 team member. However, I must make a decision by end of day today.

I understand you are extremely busy, working hard on your rebranding and new company initiatives, but it would be great if I could have some insight into whether or not you would like to move forward with my candidacy for this position.

Again, thank you for the opportunity to meet and speak with you in person. I hope to hear from you soon. Have a great day.

Sincerely,
Ismael

This placed the ball in their court, but this was something I could live with because I had an offer on the table. I had left Boston knowing I had given my all in those interviews, leaving no regrets or hidden qualities that I could have used. My reply would come a few hours later at 12:19pm stating the following:

No need to apologize! I completely understand the stress of the job search and needing answers—no need to apologize at all!

Thank you so much for coming in and meeting with us about the Digital Marketing Associate position here at Action7. It was a pleasure not only talking with you on the phone but also having the opportunity to meet you in person and introduce you to the entire team. Everyone was blown away by what you brought to the table and truly enjoyed meeting and talking with you. You left a very big impression on all of us.

At this time, we have decided to pursue another candidate, but I want to stress how truly difficult it was to make that decision. There was still hesitation about relocation and industry experience that made it a tough decision.

I wish you the best of luck with this other opportunity. Please stay in touch and don't be shy about checking in on future opportunities if you see anything posted.

Thank you again for everything. Good luck as you continue to grow your career. I am sure it will be quite impressive!

I read that email with a smile and not an ounce of disappointment. I had full understanding that ABC Marketing Incorporated is where I was to be. My faith had been restored since reconnecting with church and attending Orlando World Outreach. This was God's will.

Ismael 2009

MY JOURNEY CONTINUES...

MY ENTIRE JOURNEY THUS FAR HAS BEEN SCARY, MIND BLOWING, AND DISAPPOINTING MORE OFTEN THAN NOT. But what it proves is that I 've had the will power to fight for what I've wanted, regardless of the odds I've been up against. For the first time, I am proud of myself. I am able to stand back and congratulate myself. This feeling is refreshing, and all the weight on my shoulders has disappeared. I am now able to just close my eyes and smile for a change. I haven't allowed myself to gloat in the moment long because this is not my end nor am I anywhere close to my ultimate dreams. I've had to remember that life is a marathon, and just like everything else I've endured, I need to continue fighting through. But now my fight isn't on my own for I have an army of friends, family, and God—all of whom love me unconditionally and are ready to stand in the gap for me. I am wiser, happier and more willing to look inward, ready to work on the damage I've caused so many people.

I was determined to get out of my own way and no longer be my own worst enemy. By surrendering that title, the road has proven to be less bumpy. I no longer turn my back on my potential but now understand potential without effort is nothing but wasted opportunity. Being my own worst enemy showed me that negativity will eat you alive. It will rip you away from everything God set out for you. Life only becomes more complicated. Don't allow yourself to destroy who you were meant to be.

But first, I had to liberate my mind from a false ideal that I was a slave to perfection. Perfection was my oppressor; brainwashing me to believe its ideals were attainable. My mind was enslaved by chains of unsatisfaction combined with shackles of disappointment. I just wanted to be free. Free from this psychological warfare, free from my master, and free from myself. By acknowledging that perfection was an aim and not a destination, I gained peace of mind. Walking away from mental captivity required me to shift the perception of self away from negativity. That required me to open my ears, open my eyes, open my mind, and open my heart to consume all of this love that had my name on it. In the words of author Khalil Gibran,

> And God said, "Love your enemy," and I obeyed him and loved myself. I encourage you just to love yourself no matter how difficult of a task that may be. The rest of your life will come together—I promise.

SOURCES

WHO IS THE ENEMY?

1. Jefferson, Thomas, and William Harwood. Peden. Notes on the State of Virginia. Ed. with an Introduction and Notes by William Peden. Chapel Hill: U of North Carolina for the Institute of Early American History and Culture, 1955. N. pag. Print.

2. Lynch, William. The Willie Lynch Letter ; The Making of a Slave. Chicago, IL: Lushena, 1999. Print.

3. Lincoln, Abraham. "The Lincoln-Douglas Debates 4th Debate Part I." Lincoln-Douglas Debate. Illinois, Charleston. 18 Sept. 1858. Speech.

4. United States of America. Library of Congress. Indian Removal Act. N.p., n.d. Web. 5 Nov. 2015.

5. "Roosevelt Signs Executive Order 9066." History.com. A&E Television Networks, n.d. Web. 12 Oct. 2015.

6. "Definition of Domestic Terrorism." Uniting and Strengthening America by Providing Appropriate Tools Required to Intercept and Obstruct Terrorism (Usa Patriot Act) Act of 2001. Washington D.C.: n.p., 2012. 106. Print.

7. LoBianco, Tom. "Report: Nixon's War on Drugs Targeted Black People." CNN. Cable News Network, 23 Mar. 2016. Web. 24 Mar. 2016.

T.H.U.G. L.I.F.E.

1. Merriam-Webster. Merriam-Webster, n.d. Web. 4 Aug. 2014.

2. Shakur, Tupac Amaru. Indiana Black Expo 1993. Indiana. 4 June 2015. Speech.

3. DuBois, W.E.B. "Of Our Spiritual Strivings." The Souls of Black Folks. New York: Dodd, Mead, 1961. 3. Print.

4. "Percentage of High School Dropouts among Persons 16 through 24 Years Old (status Dropout Rate), by Sex and Race/ethnicity: Selected Years, 1960 through 2013." N.p., n.d. Web. 11 July 2015.

5. Project, The Sentencing, comp. Report of The Sentencing Project to the United Nations Human Rights Committee Regarding Racial Disparities in the United States Criminal Justice System. Publication. N.p.: n.p., n.d. Print.

DEAR DAD, I FAILED YOU

1. Kunjufu, Jawanza. "Male Seasoning and Rites of Passage." Countering The Conspiracy to Destroy Black Boys. Chicago: Afro-Am Pub., 1983. 54. Print.

CONTACT AUTHOR

Ismael Brown is a marketing consultant who lives on the edge of ideation. By channeling his thoughts, he's able to offer so much to the world that speaks far beyond his years. The trials of his life have strengthened him over time, building his character and desire to give back.

Contact the author online or via email at contact@ismaelbrown.com or at 202-455-6610

AVAILABLE ON ISMAELBROWN.COM

- Interviews with the author as he sits down to discuss the book in greater detail
- Speaking engagement booking information
- Gallery of photos of the author and his close cirlce
- Find out what the author is up to now

SOCIAL MEDIA HANDLES:

- Facebook: www.Facebook.com/Irbrown1
- Instagram: Ismael_Brown

Made in the USA
Las Vegas, NV
16 April 2022